MORE *Gems* *for the* JOURNEY

Vicki Johnson

MORE Gems for the JOURNEY

NEWSPIRIT

This body of work is to honor the center of my joy—
the Lord Jesus Christ. Everything I do is for your glory!

ACKNOWLEDGMENTS

To my daughter, parents, my spiritual parents, my siblings,
my extended family, my godchildren, KWC, Heaven 1580,
VGR, BET, and my best friends (you know who you are)—
you are my place of refuge and I love it.

Miseree Burke: *I was in church with you in the late '80s when I
received my first prophetic word from Sister McBride. She told me God
had given me the wings of an eagle so that I could rise above every storm.
I didn't understand it then. However, look what the Lord has done.
I love you so much for letting God love me through you and your family.
Thank you and I'll never forget.*

Juliet, Denise, Betty, Aleathea, and Renee:
*Thank you for helping me manage the dream.
I could not do this without you.*

Pastor Paula (Mama) Johnson: *I am TOTALLY convinced that God
put us together. We're going forward from here together
no matter what. I love you so much.* (Mom) Jeannie Marshall
and (Mom) Geraldine McInnis—
I appreciate the way you love me on your knees.

Pamela Crockett Esq., Dr. Regina Spellmon,
Marilyn (Mom) Evans, Dr. Precilla Belin, Almetra Murdock,
Lady Stacey Densmore, Mykel Trahan, Ty Adams,
Elder Evelyn Turnbull, Rev. Miriam Wright, Lady Sheila Whalum,
Pastor Sandy Maxwell, Pastor Sondra Julien,
Tracy Bethea, Renee Thompson, Megan Godley, Niambi Jarvis,
Al Collins, Sandra Chaney, Doris Cutler, Carlotta Peart,
LaWanda Forte, Stacey Stanford, Allison Brown, and
Carrie Ann Cummings—*welcome to my rainbow!
God did it and I'm grateful.*

Leona Brown, Sandra Stubbs, and Robin Wiley:
Nothing can bind you together like a hurricane, right ladies?
I love my HFC family!

To the ladies who support *I'm Every Woman*
and who attend *Girl Talk* each quarter—*you are the best audience*
a girl could have. We're in this together.

Last, but absolutely not least—Linda Gill, Glenda Howard,
Guy Chapman, Kicheko Driggins, and Selena Spencer—
thank you for embracing my gift and ensuring that
God's purpose for my life is fulfilled.

INTRODUCTION LETTER

I'm glad you made it to this point. If you read *Gems for the Journey* and are looking for more—here it is. If you are just joining us, welcome to one of God's many "transformation stations." If you read my first book and honestly embraced the process, you were stretched, challenged, provoked, encouraged and, most importantly, inspired to change. It's okay if you didn't read my first book. At some point, please read it so you can benefit from the wisdom of God that has already impacted multitudes. For now, simply get ready to exhale pain, exfoliate whatever is dead in your life and expect the best days of your life to begin right NOW.

NOW that you're here...you must continue. You made it this far and God is so proud of you. You are in a season of divine arrangements and the fact that you are reading this book is an indication that God is leaning in your direction. It's called favor. You did not make it this far to give up now. A friend of mine once told me, "God has given you grace to endure the journey until you can enjoy it." So, walk like you have a fantastic future. Live like you know your destiny is divine. Talk like you believe it's not over until God says so.

This is only possible by faith, which is the assurance of things hoped for, the proof of things we do not see and the conviction of their reality. What God is doing in your life you have never seen before. There is no reference, there is no paradigm, and there is no model. You are the first. You are authentic. You are an original. You are an example of God's intent to change the world. You are almost ready for the manifestation of something unbelievable and ridiculous. Don't worry though—even though life may look like it's working against you, in the end, it's all for your good and for His glory.

Please believe me when I say that God is up to something "tailor-made" for you. A very dear friend of mine shared with me that allowing God to heal us is not enough. After the healing, God desires to make us whole to make us ready for what He already has ready for us. Let's get moving because we have "MORE" work to do...yes, "we" have more work to do.

MORE GEMS for the JOURNEY

GEMS
for the
SPIRIT

1 *Today's Gem*

Sis, do you know you have the power to create? Yes, women are the incubators of life and the vessels God designed to bring forth children. But you have a birth canal on the opposite end of your body, too, your mouth. Your words have the power to create life or death; light or darkness; good success or bad success; victory or defeat; sickness or health. In her book, *Your Life Follows Your Words*, Darlene Bishop shares that your confession opens a door—either for God to work or for Satan to work. Honey, your miracle is in your mouth. Job 22:28 declares, "Thou shalt also decree a thing, and it shall be established unto thee: and the light shall shine upon thy ways."

Journey Note

2 *Today's Gem*

There is a line in a TLC song where they sing repeatedly, "The Girls Are Talking" and everyone knows that women can and do enjoy conversation. Proverbs 6:2 says, "You are snared with the words of your lips; you are caught by the speech of your mouth." Proverbs 15:26 says, "But the words of the pure are pleasing words to God the Father." Proverbs 21:23 states, "she who guards her mouth and her tongue keeps herself from troubles." Proverbs 12:8 declares, "The tongue of the wise brings healing." Words are important and very powerful. Jesus said in Matthew 12:37 that "our words will condemn us or make us free." Be careful what you say from this point forward—your mouth is an overflow canal of what's going on in your heart.

Journey Note

3   *Today's Gem*

Welcome to another day! God is going to complete some things in your life. He is going to tie up some loose ends. The promise of your future is going to erase the pain of your past! As women, we feel very deeply the pain associated with feeling abandoned. Whether it was a father, a husband, a boyfriend, a friend—at best it can be described as feeling left alone, frightened, empty and hopeless. But Hebrews 13:5 states, "Never will I leave you; never will I forsake you." Girl, get excited—you are never alone. You are His woman—and there is *nothing* He won't do for you!

Journey Note

4 *Today's Gem*

Psalms 139:14 declares, "I will praise you, for I am fearfully and wonderfully made. Marvelous are your works and that my soul knows very well." Okay, it's another day and you still think you should be anything but what you are. Everyone else seems to be happier, smarter, richer and better off than you. It's like they have a secret to success and you are still looking. But the answer is inside you. When you lack belief in yourself, you lack belief in God. The Father is a Master Artist and you are one of His finest creations. So embrace Hebrews 10:35–36—"Don't throw away your confidence; it will be richly rewarded. You need to persevere so that when you have done the will of God, you will receive what He has promised."

Journey Note

5   *Today's Gem*

Life is full of trauma and drama. But life is also full of love, joy and peaceful moments. Don't relinquish your right to wholeness and happiness during special occasions by focusing on what you don't have. You have so much to be thankful for. Girl, get yourself together and listen for a moment! You may not have the money to buy all the gifts you want, but you have the gift of eternal life. You may not have family to love on you — but Jesus is a friend that sticks closer than a brother and the hug you receive today is the Father's gift of love to you. Today, take a deep breath, that's a precious gift, unzip your soul and give God access to your spirit. In addition to the precious gift of His unconditional love, right now He says rest, be refreshed, be renewed, be restored!

Journey Note

6 *Today's Gem*

God is releasing revelation in the earth. This revelation knowledge is raising a Kingdom generation that is "no-nonsense." This remnant of daughters are feminine warriors with an ear to hear what the Father is saying. These warrior women have tapped into their God-given femininity and nestled into a place of intimacy that restores order. Order restores authority. Authority releases an anointing to obey God. Today, sis, do like Jesus did in John 17:1 — "Lift up your eyes to heaven and declare — Father, the hour has come." For what? For the revelation to release a revolution!

Journey Note

7 *Today's Gem*

Why are you trying to please God without faith? Hebrews 11:1 states, "Faith is the assurance of the things we hope for." Verse 6 tells us, "But without faith, it is impossible to please God. For whoever would come near to God must believe that God exists and that He is the rewarder of those who earnestly and diligently seek Him out." God has not moved and has not changed. So, why don't you believe Him when He says you are free? Why don't you trust that if you were born without it, you can live without it; without him; without them. Today, ladies, I challenge you to believe God and allow your hope to be the proof to the devil that if God said it, that settles it.

Journey Note

8 *Today's Gem*

Many of us use church as a trampoline out of our emotional and psychological valleys every week. We start from the bottom every Sunday morning, and consequently, church becomes a routine that never seems to satisfy. We expect the worship experience to lift us out of the low place we settle into—sometimes before we leave the parking lot. Thus, it's hard for us to comprehend that life can be lived in the high places ordained. Truth is, you can live in the high places of God when you expect an encounter with God on Sunday. This encounter is not just for an emotional release—it's to give you exciting revelation of who you are in Him. Habakkuk 3:19 says, "The Lord God is my strength, and He will make my feet like hinds' feet, and He will make me walk upon mine high places. Once God lifts you—keep going up."

Journey Note

9   *Today's Gem*

John 3:16 says, "For God so loved the world that He gave His only begotten Son—that whosoever believes in, trusts in, and clings to Him, should not perish but have eternal life." Jesus loves you unconditionally. His love for you is *not* based on what you've done, but on who He is. Even when He is disappointed by your behavior, He still loves you. God's love for you is perfect. Even when you mess up—He keeps on loving you. You've been accepted in the beloved. An old African proverb says, "He who conceals his disease cannot expect to be cured." Once you believe and accept that you are loved by God, you then can begin accepting and loving yourself. His love will help you turn. Turn from what? Only you know what or who that is, back to where you belong—abiding in the love of God.

Journey Note

10   *Today's Gem*

We must do the work. The word of God works if you work it. Hebrews 4:12 declares that the Word of God is quick, powerful and full of life; sharper than the sharpest dagger; it penetrates deeply, even to the dividing of soul from spirit; yes, to the inmost parts thereof. It is skilled in judging and sifts the purpose, intents and thoughts of the heart. Follow the instructions in Psalms 119:11, which instruct us to hide the word in our hearts that we might not sin against the Lord. Find a scripture, commit it to memory and watch it work wonders in your life. Remember, we must do the work.

Journey Note

11 *Today's Gem*

Yes, grace is amazing. Yes, grace is sufficient. But aren't you tired yet of God looking beyond your faults and seeing your needs? Just think how blessed you would be if God did not have to look so far to measure the contents of your obedience account. How quickly would your capacity increase if when God looked at you all He saw was obedience? Don't let grace keep you from getting better. Don't let grace stop you from doing better. Let grace and mercy be your backup while obedience takes the lead role in your life. I assure you, you can't imagine the overflow that is about to come your way.

Journey Note

12 *Today's Gem*

Isaiah 43:18–19 says, "Do not remember the former things: neither consider the things of old. Behold, I am doing a new thing! Now it springs forth: do you not perceive and know it and will you not give heed to it? I will even make a way in the wilderness and rivers in the desert." Troubled waters are not new to God—they are new to us. Unless you try something beyond what you have already mastered, you will never grow. Be comfortable with great dreams. An opportunity's favorite disguise is an obstacle. Conflict is simply a barrier on the road to your answer. Struggle is good—for it is proof that you have not quit or been conquered. The sky is not the limit—Jesus is—and in Him, there is no failure!

Journey Note

13 Today's Gem

Whenever God calls you to do the ridiculous, revelation must be your reality. Every day you must ask, "What did God say to me today?" When revelation is your reality, you live your life according to the vision and not according to the visual. Habakkuk 2:3 states to "write the vision and make it plain on tablets, that he may run who reads it. For the vision is yet for an appointed time, but at the end it will speak, and it will not lie." Write what God shows you so you won't be distracted and detoured by what you see. 2 Corinthians 5:7 reminds us to "walk by faith and not by sight." God is faithful to perform what He promised…it's just a matter of time.

Journey Note

14 *Today's Gem*

Ecclesiastes 3 says, "To everything there is a season; a time for every purpose under heaven. A time to weep and a time to laugh; a time to embrace and a time to refrain from embracing; a time to gain and a time to lose; a time to keep and a time to throw away." What season is it in your life? Is it summer and you're dressed for winter? Is it winter and you're dressed for summer? Girl, what time is it in your life? God is conditioning you for a new place. I know it's a little rough right now—but hold on, help is on the way. Galatians 6:9 says, "And let us not lose heart and grow weary and faint in doing right, for in due time and at the appointed season we shall reap if we do not relax our courage!" Again I remind you, it only takes a moment for the seasons to change.

Journey Note

15 *Today's Gem*

Psalms 63:3 declares, "Because your lovingkindness is better than life, my lips shall praise you." God alone can satisfy our deepest longings! The key is to be honest with God. Although we often try, we cannot hide from God. There is nothing covered that will not be revealed or nothing hidden that won't be known. Hebrews 4:13 says, "All things are naked and open to the eyes of Him to whom we must give account." God wants to empower you to live and not die; to prosper and not experience lack in your heart, your soul, your emotions, your mind or your spirit! God wants to fill your empty place with Himself so you can have joy — in any situation.

Journey Note

16 *Today's Gem*

There is delay, danger and often devastation in keeping what God said to destroy. God will not release the new until you bring closure to the old. You can't move forward effectively if you keep looking behind you. God wants to do a new thing in you. Even in the midst of chaos, God speaks a word of life to you today. He will make a way in the wilderness and create a flow of rivers in the desert—*just for you!* Stop rehearsing the past! Stop nursing dead issues! You can't stop the memories from coming to visit, but you don't have to invite them to stay. Let this mind be in you which was also in Christ Jesus. For when you think differently, you'll see differently! When you see differently, you'll choose differently! When you choose differently, you'll live differently. Stop trying to patch up what God said to get rid of. Matthew 9:17 says, "Put new wine into new wineskins so they both are preserved." God has something new and different for you—but first you must get rid of the old.

Journey Note

17 *Today's Gem*

Matthew 6:21 says, "For where your treasure is, there will your heart be also." Who are you in love with? Who have you given your heart to? Who has your worship? Who has your attention? Is it God who has your whole heart? Passion dominates when you are in love! The direction of your passion is the direction of your worship. The direction of your worship is the direction in which most of your time is spent. God wants to be the sail in your boat! God wants to be the wind beneath your wings! God desires to be the object of your affection. Get your affections in order. Throw all caution to the wind and give God everything...all of you. Girls, you know how we are when we fall in love! Why? Your anointing is at its peak when you get to the point that you have nothing to lose and everything to gain.

Journey Note

18   *Today's Gem*

In this season of trusting and obeying God, no longer can we reap the benefits of salvation without the responsibility of a real relationship with God. God will no longer tolerate the rituals, the routines and the religious charades. Abundance always follows obedience. Retraction of the inevitable abundance always follows disobedience. Please don't mistake God's goodness in your life as His "approval" of your choices, behavior and lifestyle if your choices, behavior and lifestyle contradict the Bible. Romans 2:4 says, "God is good to us and holds back His judgment giving us time to repent!" Listen closely, Zion is calling you to a higher place. The goodness of God is the wellspring of His glory—let Him wash you with the water of His word!

Journey Note

19 *Today's Gem*

The Bible declares in Hebrews 4:12–13, "For the word of God—the word that God speaks is alive and full of power—making it effective; it is sharper than any two-edged sword, penetrating to the dividing line of the breath of life (your soul) and the immortal (your spirit), and of joints and marrow (the deepest parts of our nature; exposing and sifting and analyzing and judging the very thoughts and purposes and intents of the heart. And not a creature exists that is concealed from His sight, but all things are open and exposed, naked and defenseless to the eyes of Him with whom we have to do." The Lord is pursuing us with the word! Let it overtake you—so it can lead you over into your promise!

Journey Note

20   *Today's Gem*

When God speaks—things happen. In Genesis 1, time and time again we read, "And God said, 'Let…'" and there was. So today, God speaks to your confusion and produces order. Today, God speaks to your distress and produces peace. Right now, God speaks to your anxiety and calls for rest. Today, God speaks to fear and converts it to faith and assurance in Him. God speaks to depression and releases unspeakable joy. Yes, God speaks to broken hearts, broken dreams and broken pieces and declares total recovery and renewed strength and courage to keep going. Today daughter of Zion, God speaks to you—"I made you in Our image and Our likeness—behold, it is very good and I have approved you completely." In Him, you are already blessed—now live like it!

Journey Note

21 *Today's Gem*

Praise is the language of love. It communicates to the recipient how much they are adored, admired, acknowledged and appreciated. Praise is the prelude to the more intimate experience of worship. Worship takes place "beyond the veil." It costs to go behind the veil. Whether it's the veil to enter the "holy of holies" or the veil to enter the most sacred place of your womanhood—the price is still the same. The cost is "commitment!" So increase your ability to commune with God by adding "praise" to the languages you speak. Now that you're bilingual, expect an increase in your capacity to receive more of God!

Journey Note

22 *Today's Gem*

Are you Mary or Martha? Like Martha, are you so busy doing church work, serving others, impressing others, caring for others that you have neglected to make time and just sit at His feet? God believes in priorities. He honors women who make time for Him first; then themselves; then their families; then ministry. Are you busy due to full devotion to God or man? Listen, the word *no* is a part of the Kingdom language. It's okay. Seek God to establish or reestablish what's really important! With God, we accomplish more, when *we* work less.

Journey Note

23 *Today's Gem*

It's time for you to come forth! What are you waiting for? Who are you waiting for? Why? Could it be that you have failed to realize that you *already* have everything you need to move forward. The greater one is in you! I John 4:4 declares, "You belong to God and have already defeated the enemy, because He who lives in you is mightier and more powerful than he who is in the world." Take inventory and take action. You've already prayed about it—now *be* about it! This is your due season! Your water has broken, your labor has begun—*now push!*

Journey Note

24 *Today's Gem*

God honors humility! James 4:10 says, "Humble yourselves in the sight of the Lord and He will lift you up." The way down is up! Position yourself like the woman with the alabaster box—at the feet of Jesus. Humility is a prerequisite to ruling and reigning with Christ. Walking in humility is a heart issue, a lifestyle and a mentality. Yield your heart to the supernatural impartation of the Lord so that you become a garment of humility—available for the Lord's display! Likewise, the Lord delights in your contentment with the hidden treasures between you and Himself! Lord, make me a fragrance to you and to those I encounter today! I only want what you want for my life!

Journey Note

25 Today's Gem

Christian author Watchman Nee said, "When God opens our eyes that we may know the intent of our heart and the deepest thought within us in the measure that He, Himself, knows us—that's revelation. As we are naked and laid bare before Him, so are we before ourselves as we receive revelation. This is revelation: for us to be allowed to see what God sees!" What does God see when He looks at us? He sees Himself. Therefore, cancel the pity party. You are fearfully and wonderfully made! You are the righteousness of God in Christ Jesus. You are the head and not the tail. You are healed, you are whole and you already have worth. It's time for you to get up, shake the dust off and get moving. God has great plans for you because He is great. There is not an issue you can have, woman, that God can't handle. What you are going through is not about where you are—it's about where you are going! Now get moving…God is waiting there to blow your mind.

Journey Note

26 *Today's Gem*

Dr. Mark Hanby says that God's order of breaking bread is to take it, bless it, break it and then give it. Today, God wants you to know that your brokenness is a part of the process of God expanding you. He took you from something, blessed you and now He is breaking you. In the midst of brokenness, ungodly pleasures become painful. Brokenness draws you back into the will of God because self-will and brokenness do not get along. In the midst of brokenness, God gives us what we need—not always what we want. Brokenness is God's friend. Any friend of God is a friend of yours! So in the midst of this broken place, let everything go—before God gives you to be multiplied, He will give back what belongs to you.

Journey Note

27 *Today's Gem*

Who is like the Lord? Our desire should be to become like Him. The character of God is multifaceted. Unless we are prepared to study every facet, we will always have a distorted view of Him. In the words of Joy Dawson, "God is something like a giant diamond. His true, intrinsic beauty will only be seen by those who take time to have a close-up, concentrated focus on the wonders of His whole personhood." God wants to ruin you to the ordinary. He wants to captivate you with His majesty, His mystery and His meekness. He wants to be the lover of your soul. Do yourself a favour and pursue Him with your whole heart…you will be so glad you did.

Journey Note

28 *Today's Gem*

In a culture filled with microwaves, fast-food restaurants and drive-thru banking, it can be very difficult to "wait." Faith Tibbetts McDonald said in her article "Finding Worth In Your Wait" that waiting can be grueling and sometimes, waiting can be cruel. When waiting seems to never end, we must look beyond our circumstances and trust God with the outcome. God's purpose is always fulfilled in our waiting. Sometimes waiting builds character; other times it's God's way of giving us much needed rest. Waiting is one of God's ways to teach us patience. Possessing the virtue of patience is a sign of spiritual maturity. James 1:4 says, "Let patience have its perfect work, that you may be perfect and complete, lacking nothing." God has a message for you in your wait—listen closely. He wants to tell you something that's worth waiting for!

Journey Note

29 *Today's Gem*

Are you eyeball-to-eyeball with destiny and can't touch it? Are you like the children of Israel—you can see the promised land, but you can't get to it? You've made it this far and can't move, huh? Well, it's not elephants that trample on our dreams. The Bible tells us in Song of Solomon that it is the "little foxes that spoil the vine." Today's fox is unforgiveness. Unforgiveness always keeps you from reaching the mark—no matter how close you are. Unforgiveness affects your body (the stress manifests as different ailments), it affects your soul (it numbs your emotions and stifles your worship) and it affects your spirit (it kills your communication with God). The key to your release is to separate the offense from the offender. Let the power of the Holy Ghost empower you to forgive the offense—God will give you grace to deal with the offender! My spiritual father, Bishop Ralph Dennis taught me that...thanks, Dad.

Journey Note

30 *Today's Gem*

The Bible commands us in Philippians 4:6–7 "to be not anxious or worry about anything, but in every circumstance, by prayer and thanksgiving, continue to make what we need known to God. And God's peace, which transcends all understanding, shall be yours and will guard your heart and mind in Christ Jesus!" Worrying cannot add a single hour to your life. You can overcome worry by resting near the quiet waters in Psalm 23. Max Lucado painted the picture so vividly when he said, "God isn't behind us yelling 'Go!' He's ahead of us bidding us to 'Come!' He's in front, clearing the path, and just before the curve God says, 'Turn here,' and prior to the rise He says, 'step up here.'" God's help is always timely. He has placed Himself between us and what concerns us. At the right time, He gives us direction. Yes, He may not come when we think we need Him, but He is always—on time!

Journey Note

31 Today's Gem

God wants you to tap into your pearl-producing power. How? Decide to live a life that pleases the Lord in all respects. From the time you wake up in the morning to the time you go to bed at night, set your heart's desire on exalting Him. When the Spirit of God prompts you to do something, give expression to that impression. Don't ignore it. Seek to obey the leading of the Lord on a moment-by-moment basis. Ephesians 5:18 says to "be filled with the Spirit." In order to be full of God, you must first be empty of self. God wants all of you. You can settle for being an imitation by trying to cover ungodly character or you can allow the Holy Spirit to use the sands of "process" to create the real thing.

Journey Note

32 *Today's Gem*

Francis Bacon said, "The best part of beauty is that which no picture can express." I just love being a woman—don't you? In her book, *Keep It Simple For Busy Women*, Emily Barnes said that woman are more than lace and flowers. We are called to be women after God's own heart. Women with teachable hearts who can give and forgive, protect and respect, manage and multiply. It is possible—we can go with ease, from craze to praise. Today, pray that your life will flow with God's love and peace. Pray that as women of God we move by His Spirit and with His joy! Take the love of God and wrap it around every task you do today and every person you encounter. Our privilege is to fill our homes with prayer, peace and pleasure. That's the beautiful gift that comes with the spirit of femininity! Celebrate the treasure of womanhood.

Journey Note

33 *Today's Gem*

Are you a woman of virtue or a simple sista? Virtue is developed over time as you allow the Spirit of God to do a special work in your life. It is the Spirit of God, not you, who produces godly character. God wants to make you as a string of pearls. These pearls of character are found in Galatians 5:22–23 and are known as love, joy, peace, patience, kindness, goodness, faithfulness, gentleness and self-control. As these qualities develop, your life will become like a beautiful necklace strung with the pearls of godly character. Simple sistas adorn themselves with immorality, sensuality, jealousy, idolatry and constant disputes, to name a few. If you have a bad bead on your string of pearls, remove it and replace it with a quality that pleases God.

Journey Note

34 Today's Gem

Love on yourself today. You are worthy of love. Love multiplies, not divides. Love is patient. Love is kind. Love adds to you and causes you to grow. Love constrains you to be drawn to "character," not cosmetics. Love empowers you to abide where you are truly celebrated—not haphazardly tolerated. Love is what love does—it is an action word. Love provokes you to change for the better. Love doesn't take advantage of your weakness—love covers you while God works on you. Oh, in case you missed it—God is love. So it is really God that multiplies, adds, empowers, provokes and covers you. What's love got to do with it? God has everything to do with it.

Journey Note

35   *Today's Gem*

Today is your day, Queen! Purpose in your heart to walk like royalty. Be mindful of your conversations and talk like royalty. Look good. Sound good. Be all that God said you are—even if your immediate circumstances don't reflect what He said. Know this. If God said it, that settles it, and His word confirms it. Isaiah 55:11 says, "So shall my word be that goes forth out of my mouth; it shall not return to me void or useless. It shall accomplish that which I please and purpose, and it shall prosper in the thing for which I sent it." Celebrate Christ in you…the hope of glory. Celebrate the dreams that are about to come to pass in your life because it is due season. Declare it to be so. Proverbs 18:21 says you've got the power to do so!

Journey Note

36 *Today's Gem*

Hey, Sis—you are not alone! God wants you to know that it is not as bad as you think it is. It could be so much worse. God wants to lift you up and out of that "well of depression." He wants you to know that you are empowered to walk from under that cloud and into the Sonshine…S-O-N shine. In the Son, your vision is clearer. In the Son, your pathway is brighter. In the Son, you feel the warmth of His love. In the Son, "God gives you beauty for ashes, the oil of joy for mourning, and the garment of praise for the spirit of heaviness." Whatever you do…don't quit. Rest in the Lord and wait patiently for Him. Then, address the "life issues" that have brought you to this place. With God, nothing is impossible. This storm did not come to kill you. It came to make you stronger! Remember, it is in the midst of your weakness that you have access to His strength!

Journey Note

37 Today's Gem

What is it that is keeping you from loving Jesus first? Who is it that has come between you and the lover of your soul? Are you too busy? Busyness is a trick of the devil to keep you distracted. In Christ, you work less but you accomplish more. Often, we as women substitute "church work" for the "work of the church." Perhaps we have become too busy putting our religion on display to impress others that we have lost perspective on what is most important—an enriching and deep, love relationship with the Lord. Barbara James said it this way—"We will not reach for more until we are dissatisfied with our current level of relationship." Mediocrity is an enemy of excellence. Even if it is good—it could be better. Allow God to stretch you past your fears and natural inabilities. You will be surprised at the new adventures you encounter in Christ.

Journey Note

38 *Today's Gem*

The Bible says in Job 22:21, "Acquaint now yourself with Him; agree with God and show yourself to be conformed to His will and be at peace. By that, you shall prosper and great good shall come to you." We know many things about God—but do we know God? God wants to "know you" in an intimate way. In the midst of intimacy there is conception and consequent birthing. Keep your relationship with God in a mode of intimacy. Keep Him near you. God wants to show you another side of Himself. He wants to be your provider, your defender, your confidant and your true love. Not only do you get acquainted with God, but in the spirit of peace, great good shall come to you.

Journey Note

39 Today's Gem

Are you so caught up in the "what-ifs" of the future that you are missing the beauty and the blessing of the "right now"? Nothing about your life as a believer is an accident. God has a reason for requiring your patience. I Thessalonians 5:18 says, "In everything give thanks; for this is the will of God in Christ Jesus for you." This is the season of trusting and obeying God. If you are willing to be at peace with the pace of God in your life, He is willing to give you His very best for your life. God's sovereign will is always meant for your good and for His glory. Proverbs 3:5–6 admonishes us "to trust in the Lord with all our heart and lean not to your own understanding; in all your ways acknowledge Him, and He will direct your path." The moment you find contentment with where you are is the moment of your release into God's "next" for your life.

Journey Note

40   *Today's Gem*

Are you in church but out of Christ? God wants you to know today that there is no peaceful coexistence with the devil. There are some things in your life that you must destroy for your future success in Christ. Yes, in Christ is where your success lies. God is not going to change His plans for your life to accommodate your vision. God will not share your heart with other idols. When Jesus becomes your *everything*, He automatically evicts people and things that do not belong. God is the ultimate significant other—no matter what your status is. This walk is not about religion, but about relationship. Release Him to be God in your life. If you made it this far, Sis, you can make it the rest of the way.

Journey Note

41 *Today's Gem*

The devil does not want you to hear this. But it's too late. Romans 8:1–2 declares, "There is therefore now no condemnation to those who are in Christ Jesus, who live not and walk not after the dictates of the flesh, but after the dictates of the Spirit. For the law of the Spirit of life which is in Christ Jesus has set you free from the law of sin and death." You are *free!* You are not that woman anymore. You are *free!* You are released to pursue God. You are *free!* What you did is not who you are. You are the righteousness of God. You are full of joy because God said so! If the devil can keep you guilty, he can keep you defeated. People who magnify other people's faults do so to avoid facing their own shortcomings. The moment you realize their words have no power over you—you are free of their opinions. The devil is no different. Confuse him with your praise. Worry him with your worship of the Lord Jesus Christ. Why? Because you are not coming out of *this* the same way you went in! You went in bound, but you are coming out *free!*

Journey Note

42 *Today's Gem*

In his book, *Choosing God's Best*, author Don Raunikar said that it takes faith and courage to wait on God. Waiting for the Lord means pausing for further instructions yet continuing to worship and serve Him with your whole heart. We get in trouble when we make decisions impulsively, without waiting for God's timing and God's thinking because Satan takes legitimate needs and tempts us to meet those needs in illegitimate ways. God has a reason for requiring your patience. Psalms 27:14 admonishes us to "wait, hope for and expect the Lord; be brave and of good courage and let your heart be strong and enduring. Yes, wait for and expect the Lord." God understands our need not to be alone. While you wait—worship, for He has plans to prosper you, not to harm you, to give you a hope and a future.

Journey Note

43 Today's Gem

When I was a little girl, one of my favorite games was hide-and-seek. I think that game has survived down through the years because it is so easy to learn. I found it more interesting that even "hiding" began in the book of Genesis. In Genesis 3:8, "Adam and Eve hid themselves from the presence of the Lord God among the trees of the garden" because of disobedience. Today, some of us are still playing hide-and-seek with God. Our disobedience has caused us to realize our nakedness, be ashamed of our nakedness, and hide our nakedness from the one who is waiting to cover us with His love. God has finished his countdown…ready or not here He comes. Just like He called out to Adam, He is calling out to you. Are you available to be found or are you going to keep running?

Journey Note

44 *Today's Gem*

Some roadblocks are not the devil. It's God trying to get your attention. Anytime you go against God you'll run into Him. Why? It's impossible to run into God if you are running with God. Remember, sis, your steps are ordered by God, so slow down and enjoy the journey. Don't be in such a rush to get there. There are lessons learned along the way and the treasures are gathered as you go. Relax and trust God to get you there on time. He's never late.

Journey Note

45 *Today's Gem*

Proverbs 18:24 says, "Jesus is a friend that sticks closer than a brother." Too often after experiencing a broken heart, we as women build walls to attempt to protect ourselves from ever feeling that kind of pain again. Consequently, no love can come out, and conversely, no love can come in—not even the love of Christ. This same fear of pain keeps us from surrendering our hearts completely to the Lord. But what you need to understand is that love is not something that God gives and takes away. He is love! He is motivated by love to constrain me into a relationship with Him. His goodness draws me. His kindness keeps me. He favor sustains me. His power protects me. His shadow covers me in the midst of warfare and causes me to be at rest. Do you want to know what love is? Well God wants to show you—open up your heart and let Him in.

Journey Note

46 *Today's Gem*

Get up and get moving because the Lord says so! You cannot stay here where you are. You have too much to do and you've got too much to lose. Isaiah 40 says, "Have you not known? Have you not heard? The everlasting God, the Lord, the Creator of the ends of the earth, does not faint or grow weary; there is no searching of His understanding. He gives power to the faint and weary, and to her who has no might, He increases strength (causing it to multiply and making it to abound). But those who wait for the Lord and hope in Him, shall change and renew their strength and power; they shall lift their wings and mount up close to God as eagles; they shall run and not get weary, they shall walk and not faint." You have the power to change your situation—how bad do you want to?

Journey Note

47 Today's Gem

The wind of God is blowing and church as usual is over. Church is simply the gateway to the third dimension of glory or the Kingdom of God. If you've got good religion, then that is your problem. For religion is man's interpretation of God and is not sufficient to propel you into wholeness. What you need is a real relationship directly with Jesus Christ. Relationship involves truth, honesty and love. Religion keeps you bound—relationship sets you free. Religion abuses and misuses you—relationship heals and comforts you. Religion stifles your growth—relationship matures and expands your territory. Religion is man's idea—relationship is God's ideal. Do you want to enter the most holy place of God? Then begin to confront your issues and be released into a place you have never imagined.

Journey Note

48 *Today's Gem*

Too often we want to write the script for our lives and offer our plans to God as if they were His blueprints. However, the patterns of the Lord are consistent. The number three denotes completion, fullness, wholeness and perfection. The Bible tells us in Romans 12:2 that "we are to be transformed by the renewing of our minds so that we may prove what is that good (the first dimension of glory), and acceptable (the second dimension of glory), and perfect (third dimension of glory) will of God." In the *good* place, we follow our ideas, our plans. In the *acceptable* place, we live with the reality that we created. But in the *perfect* place, we allow God to invade, and interrupt our frustrated existence to thrust us into His ideal situation for our lives. Who designed your present location?

Journey Note

49 Today's Gem

My Father in the Lord, Bishop Ralph Dennis, was preaching about "a deeper place" and he said that "God wants to break your routine and cast you into the unusual." I know you like tradition. But tradition is the *living faith of dead men*. I know it's easier for you to operate with a mentality of traditionalism. But traditionalism is the *dead faith of living men*. Heretofore, the Body of Christ has been bound by man's opinion, interpretation and execution of rules and regulations that have nothing to do with Kingdom manifestation. *God has no grandchildren!* Each generation must get to know Him personally. How well do your know your Father?

Journey Note

50 *Today's Gem*

Change is coming! God is shaking the earth and everything that is not rooted and grounded in His love will fall away. God is calling us back to "holiness" and "wholeness." Holiness is not a denomination, but a lifestyle. Holiness is not based on the way you dress, but the condition of your heart. Holiness is not just what you say, but how you think and consequently how you act. Holiness is love, joy, peace, long-suffering, gentleness, temperance, faith, goodness and meekness. Deuteronomy 30 commands us to choose between life and death. Don't just make a good choice, make a God choice and get ready to walk into your promise!

Journey Note

51   *Today's Gem*

I feel led to push my sistas through this transition you are in. God is calling you to a "deeper place." My Pastor, Bishop Ralph Dennis, calls this place both "crucial" and "painful." It's crucial because you cannot afford to miss it, and it is painful because of what is required of you. When you pursue the will of God for your life, He interrupts and intrudes your plans to bring forth His purpose. The Lord is stretching you and making you uncomfortable where you are because He has plans for you. He is calling you to dwell in the secret place of the Most High. He is calling you close to reveal some things to you about you that amaze you! I know, you've heard that before—but you need to hear it until you believe it. You are an amazing woman and God has great plans for you.

Journey Note

52 Today's Gem

Everybody's talking about "No More Drama"—including me! Drama is the result of not putting the devil in his place. I Peter 5:8 tells us "to be sober, be vigilant, for your adversary the devil, walks about like a roaring lion seeking whom he may devour." The devil is after your purpose, your peace, your promise, your power and your praise. Let me give you a little nugget—drama and the devil are synonymous! If you want to understand your drama, then you need to get an understanding of the devil! James 4:7 says, "Submit to God, resist the devil and he will flee from you." Likewise, submit to God, resist the "drama" and it will disappear.

Journey Note

53   *Today's Gem*

You are in the valley of decision. You are in between *never again* and *never before*. It's called transition. Transition is a strange place. Transition is the vehicle God uses to shift you into the next dimension of purpose in your life. Transition shatters your illusions and disrupts your ability to continue living in drama. Transition teaches you things about yourself that you did not know. How? Transition often leads you to the wilderness and there—you come face to face with God. When God speaks—things happen. This pivotal encounter launches you into a place you've never been before—the outer limits of God! Here you must choose God and multiply or be drawn away and surely die! Now what? You choose!

Journey Note

54   *Today's Gem*

Matthew 28:20 declares, "Lo, I am with you always, perpetually and on every occasion, to the close and consummation of the age." He was there when you were born. He was there when you played with your dolls. He was there when you entered womanhood. He was there when you made your mistakes. He was there when you messed up. He was there in the midnight hour when no one else was available to hear your pain or see your tears. He was there when you envisioned your future. He was there as you pursued your future. He is there with you right now. He will be there in your future, for Exodus 3:14 declares, "I am who I am and what I am, and I will be what I will be." In other words, He is the future!

Journey Note

55 *Today's Gem*

God is at His best when He does not make sense. Have you ever been in a strange place? It's a place between where you have been and where you are going. The waiting period comes to qualify and certify you for the promise. God is not arbitrary in His plans for you. In Isaiah 46:10, "God declares the end from the beginning and because He spoke it, He will do it." God has a set time for you. Isaiah 30:18 puts it this way— "Blessed are those who wait for Him!" Wait with patience and undisturbed composure on the promises of God in your life. Once you pass the test of waiting, what's yours is coming to you!

Journey Note

56 *Today's Gem*

God is still in the giving business. Today He wants you to know that the more you love, the more you praise. Praise paralyzes the devil. In the midst of praise, a conversion takes place and your weakness becomes strength, your sorrow becomes joy, your turmoil becomes peace and your lack becomes more than enough. When you allow God to increase your capacity to love, it increases your capacity to praise—an increased capacity to praise, increases your capacity to become more like Him. The more you become like Him, the more you increase! Once you shift toward more, don't look back—you are about to encounter your moment of release!

Journey Note

57 *Today's Gem*

The Bible says in Romans 10:17 that "faith comes by hearing, and hearing by the word of God." Too many of us have wimpy faith. When it comes to trusting God, we don't put ourselves out there because we're not really sure He'll come through for us. Sis, if you live on low faith, it's because you don't spend enough time in God's word. Do you want to grow your faith? If so, rearrange your priorities, take better control of your time and read the bible. His word strengthens you for tough times. Live in such a way that God has to come through for you—live by His word.

Journey Note

58   *Today's Gem*

God is not in the business of fulfilling dreams He didn't give you. Psalms 37:4 declares, "Delight yourself also in the Lord and He shall give you the desires of your heart." This means that as you purpose to live a life that pleases God, God will then plant in your heart the things He has in store for you. Wow! What an awesome position to hold in the Kingdom—the more you please God the more purpose He unveils in your life. The more you allow Him to unveil, the more pleased He is…and it keeps going and going and going.

Journey Note

59   *Today's Gem*

Stop living beneath your privilege and begin living like the heir you are. Salvation comes with a benefits package. Psalm 103 declares, "Bless the Lord, oh my soul, and all that is within me bless His holy name. Bless the Lord, oh my soul, and forget not *all* His benefits. Who forgiveth all thine iniquities (that's salvation from sin); who healeth all they diseases (that's healing from sickness); who redeemeth thy life from destruction (that's deliverance and protection); who crowneth thee with lovingkindness and tender mercies; who satisfieth they mouth with good things so that thy youth is renewed like the eagle's (that's preservation and wholeness)." Did you get it? We are saved, healed, delivered, protected, preserved, and whole—that's your right. Now live like it.

Journey Note

60   *Today's Gem*

Somebody listening today has been hiding from God on the front line. You are on the front line of a war that has already been won on your behalf. But if you don't respond to the call of God to come forth and come clean, you must face the consequence of that decision and you run the risk of being exposed. You can fool the people that you're standing beside, but you can't fool God. His love wants to heal you from that spirit of deception. Exodus 15:26 declares, "If you will diligently hearken to the voice of the Lord your God, and will do what is right in His sight—and if you will listen and obey His commandments and keep all His statutes, He will not put on you none of the diseases brought upon the Egyptians, for I am the Lord Who heals you." You can't just be for Him with your mouth. God wants your mind, your heart and your lifestyle.

Journey Note

61 *Today's Gem*

Joann Rosario has a song entitled "More, More, More" describing her hunger to receive more of God. Well, today, God is issuing an invitation to you to receive more. He wants to give you more love. 1 Corinthians 12:31 says "to earnestly desire the best gift. And yet I will still show you a more excellent way—the highest gift of all—which is love." For when you walk in love, you are free to be who God says you are because it connects you to wholeness, which frees you to love others the way God loves you—unconditionally. John 3:16 says that "For God so loved the world that He gave…" Today, He is still giving and He wants to give you more.

Journey Note

62 *Today's Gem*

Looking at our circumstances without filtering what we see through the eyes of faith can cause us as women to be insecure. Of course it is very difficult to admit that we are not sure we can trust God to give us what we desire. In our minds, that admission is an indication to others that we are weak in our faith. God knows when our hearts ache for things that are precious to us. But He also knows that earthly things will not make us secure. Faith does not eliminate questions. But faith knows where to take them. Spend some quality time reading the Word of God aloud. For Romans 10 tells us that "faith comes by hearing, and hearing by the Word of God." Speak the Word, woman of faith, and your vision will become clearer.

Journey Note

63   *Today's Gem*

Sis, your season of lack is over. You are being positioned for multiple streams of wealth. I'm not just talking about money, either. Wealth includes relationships, peace of mind, unspeakable joy, divine health, emotional well-being and unshakable faith. Don't worry about any deficits in these areas, they are simply distractions. God is ready to do in your life what people thought was impossible. Yes, it has been a season of great testing—and now it's your season to manifest great results. This place of wealth has been calling your name—respond today!

Journey Note

64 Today's Gem

Too often we cover who we are with what we do. We hide our weaknesses by learning to be something we are not. Are you living a lie trying to hide the real, true you? Do you hide behind the facade of a public image? If so, come out, come out—wherever you are! Come out from behind the veil of shame, and the cloak of guilt. You have not survived all that you have been through for it to end like this! Jesus is looking for that "little girl" who has learned to mask her pain with a smile. He wants to rescue you from drowning in the sea of "I can't" and carry you to the safety of "I can do all through Christ who strengthens me." Lazarus is not the only one who Jesus called forth! He is calling you back to life right now.

Journey Note

65 Today's Gem

The place where the devil thought he destroyed you is the place where God starts to use you. God never calls you by your situation. He calls you by the promise and purpose attached to your life. If you hear someone calling you by your situation, then you know that is not God speaking to you. God looks at you and sees Himself! Consequently, God is trying to move you from where you are, to what He has for you. The pulling, the pushing, the stretching, the squeezing — that is God making you ready for what He already has ready for you. Today, God is separating your past from your present, and connecting your present to your future. Trust God! If you have made it this far, you can make it the rest of the way!

Journey Note

66 *Today's Gem*

God still desires to know you! In spite of your past experiences, your present circumstances and your potential drama that is waiting in the wings for an opening, God wants to know you and He wants you to know Him. Satan's first attack upon the human race was his sly effort to destroy Eve's confidence in the kindness of God. The devil has continued to lie to Eve's daughters. As a result, fear has often alienated women from the One who loves them as they need to be loved. Deep within a woman's soul remains the longing for the gentle embrace of the God who is, not the God the enemy has deceived us into seeking. When you love someone, you give them your whole heart, the center of your being and the essence of who you are. God asks for no less. He is calling you today to slip under His wings of love and discover for yourself who He really is.

Journey Note

67 *Today's Gem*

You are the apple of God's eye! Daddy's girl. With all of your issues—you are still loveable! With all of your hang-ups, you are already valuable! So from this point on, act like you deserve God's best! Why? Because your Father is a King—that makes you a princess. Now, plan for your future—but enjoy your present. Value your intuition and wisdom. Develop healthy, supportive relationships. Make forgiveness a priority— please do this. Unforgiveness is holding up your destiny. I know you feel you have a right to hold on to it. But the reality is that unless you release the offense and trust God to help you forgive the offender—they are wounding you AGAIN!!! Receive this spirit of release today and let go of everything and everybody that stands between you and your Kingdom destiny. This is your season to reign, my sister! Not according to your plans, but scripted by God's sovereignty!

Journey Note

68 *Today's Gem*

The *International Children's Bible* describes faith this way in Hebrews 11:1: "Faith means being sure of the things we hope for. And faith means knowing that something is real even if we do not see it." This child-like expression of such an abstract quality can become your daily reality as a woman of faith. Your hope cannot be put in some dreamed-up future that you have planned. Your hope must be in the God who knows your past, present and future, and who loves you enough to give you the best. Are you in a no-hope situation? I know you want to please God—therefore, reconsider your circumstances and realize that what seems like a hopeless situation is just the view from the other side of where God is about to take you.

Journey Note

69 *Today's Gem*

You are not a mistake! Yes, you make mistakes—but *you* are not a mistake. God does not make mistakes. In Genesis 1:31, "God saw everything that He had made and behold, it was very good (suitable and pleasant) and He approved it completely." Your life is a symphony with many different instruments such as pain, trouble, distress, tragedy, illness, loss and betrayal. The good news is, every symphony orchestra has a conductor to bring it all together to sound beautiful. So, to every "Queen" that is listening—Jesus is the conductor of the concert of your life, and although individually, each instrument may not be that appealing, the finished product is a masterpiece!

Journey Note

70 *Today's Gem*

Get in touch with the Father's heart. For therein lies the revelation of who you are in Christ and who Christ is in you. When you touch the Father's heart, you find love, peace, joy, acceptance, affirmation and wholeness. When you touch the Father's heart, you find power—not just a form of godliness. When you touch the Father's heart you find hope, healing and happiness. When you touch the Father's heart, you find that no one can love you like He can—for the love of God is the perfection of affection. Once you touch the Father's heart, you'll never settle for less than God's best and like Stephanie Mills, you'll be singing—"I Never Knew Love Like This Before!"

Journey Note

71 *Today's Gem*

Ladies, what do you do when your heart's desire is not God's will? Proverbs 3:5 tells us to lean on, trust in and be confident in the Lord with all your heart and mind, and do not rely on your own insight and understanding. When your heart's desire conflicts with the Word of God—choose the Word! Don't make a good choice—make a God choice. Hide the word in your heart so you won't sin against God. The key to spiritual discipline is staying with what you know and not going with you feel. Pray and ask God to give you His heart—then you will know your motives are right in line with God's purpose for your life. If you believe what you ask, you will respond like you have it.

Journey Note

72 Today's Gem

Patiently wait for the promise! Anything born too soon is premature and runs the risk of developmental disabilities. Premature birth has a tremendous expense attached to it. Likewise, when we push too soon in the things of God, we run the risk of experiencing complications that God never purposed for our lives. Are you driving your purpose or is purpose driving you? Hebrews 11:35–36 commands us to "not cast away our confidence, for it carries a great and glorious reward. For you have need of patience and endurance, so that you may perform and fully accomplish the will of God—and thus receive and enjoy to the fullest—what is promised."

Journey Note

73   *Today's Gem*

Go on in the name of the Lord! Too often, we allow other people's opinion—of us, about us, to us—to determine if we are going to obey God or not. Well, guess what? Go on whether they go with you or not. Go on, whether they affirm you or not. Go on, whether they agree with you or not. *Choose to obey what God has declared about you!* I know they can't forget what they know about your past—but what you did is not who you are. Ephesians 1:6 says that "you are accepted in the beloved." *Girl, you've got it going on!* Let the devil know from this day forward, it's not your fault; it's just your turn to walk in the favor of God. This is your season— in spite of what it looks like—by faith, believe that God is about to blow your mind right through here, right through here! Go on in the name of the Lord.

Journey Note

74 *Today's Gem*

For the joy that is set before you—endure the cross! Jesus did in Hebrews 12:2 and now He is seated at the right hand of Father. Endure the discomfort of transition for it is a wisdom-gaining and maturing process. Endure the loneliness of being separated from the familiar—for God is stretching your capacity to receive more of Him. Endure the silence of having no one to talk to—God is teaching you to hear His voice. The sooner you submit to your cross, the sooner you will be resurrected. Be encouraged Great Woman of God—for on the other side of this opposition is a tremendous opportunity that will change your life! It only takes one day for the seasons to change!

Journey Note

75   *Today's Gem*

It's D-Day! Don't worry though—the battle has already been won. The devil is launching his missiles of deception, depression, disappointment, denial, discouragement, doubt, distractions, disease and dysfunction. But 2 Corinthians 2:14 says, "Thanks be to God which *always* causes us to triumph in Christ." Today be a graceful warrior! Your weapons of choice are deliverance, determination, destiny, diligence and your dreams. Devastate the enemy of your soul with your desire to please God. Deny access to anything that pulls you out of place. Declare what has been written about you in eternity! Delight yourself in the Lord! Life and death is in the power of the tongue and you have been commissioned to speak those things that be not as though they were!

Journey Note

76 *Today's Gem*

Our eyesight is the number one source of stimuli to the brain. We receive 80 per cent of our information through what we see. That is why blindness is so devastating to a person's ability to function independently. Likewise in the spirit, what we see through the eyes of faith determine our ability to navigate challenges. 2 Corinthians 5:7 tells us, "For we walk by faith and not by sight." It is the devil's job to keep truth hidden from you. Therefore, he blinds us with disappointment, discouragement and disarray. This is why we keep bumping into barriers in our lives—because our spiritual eyes of faith are handicapped. Do you want to please God? Then activate your faith. Release your spiritual walking stick of fear. Through your eyes of faith—see yourself free! See your future in the past tense so that it can become your now. Know this—your faith has already made you whole.

Journey Note

77 *Today's Gem*

Are you blessed and highly favored? Of course you are! But today God wants to add flavor to your favor. The favor is for you—the flavor is for others. Matthew 5:13 says, "You are the salt of the earth, but if the salt has lost its taste—then it is good for nothing." What are you good for today? Are you prepared to sprinkle joy in a sad place? What about a dash of love where there is hatred? Can God count on you today for a pinch of light in a dark place? Or are you so consumed with your favor that you can't recognize the needs of others. You are blessed to be a blessing! You are healed to help somebody else. You are anointed to change situations, places and people. There is life in you to give away. The best part of it is that you don't have to do anything but show up and smile. God will show off through you—if you let Him!

Journey Note

78 *Today's Gem*

Several years ago many believers starting asking "What would Jesus do?" when confronted with various quagmires and situations. But to ask that question is to ask yourself—am I really ready for the answer? Why? Quite often, the answer will require you to grow or expand beyond your comfort zone. To follow Christ requires a commitment. Commitments either develop you or destroy you. Either way, commitments define you. Every single choice you make has consequences so choose wisely. Christlikeness is the result of making Christlike choices. Listen, sis, God accurately reproduces His character in you when your choices honor Him.

Journey Note

79 Today's Gem

Colossians 3:16 says, "Let the words of Christ enrich your life by living in your heart and mind to make you rich, wise and full of insight." Many of us suffer from spiritual malnutrition and it shows when a crisis occurs in our lives. For your soul and spirit to prosper and be healthy, God's word *must* become your first priority. To embrace this truth, women of God, is to live. To hear it and ignore it, is to set yourself up for failure and frustration. God's word must be the counsel for making decisions and the reference for evaluating relationships. Stop making choices based on culture (everyone's doing it); tradition (we've always done it this way); or emotion (it just feels right). These are flawed authorities. God's word is flawless and will *never* lead you in the wrong direction.

Journey Note

80 *Today's Gem*

God does not want a religious, ritualistic relationship with you. He desires an intimate heart-to-heart, transforming friendship with each of us. Psalms 42:1–2 says, "As the deer pants and longs for the water brook, so my soul longs and pants for you, O God. My inner self thirsts for God, for the living God." Too often in our rush to perform for God, we fail to simply enjoy His company. Enjoying His company means you seek, long for, thirst for, wait for, see, know, love, hear and respond to God. Set aside quality time to work on your relationship with God. It's a journey you will never forget and a gift you won't want to return.

Journey Note

81 *Today's Gem*

Temptation needs your cooperation to complete its mission. Temptation has no respect for wisdom and is specialized in making its victims forsake knowledge, wise counsel and common sense. But God's word *never* changes. 1 Corinthians 10:13 says, "For no temptation—no matter how it comes—has overtaken you that is not common to man or beyond human resistance." But God is faithful to His word and He won't allow you to be tempted beyond your ability to resist and endure, and will always provide a way out. In other words, we are without excuse. Choose God, girlfriend, and be blessed!

Journey Note

82 Today's Gem

Compromise is never worth it. In reality, most of what we compromise for only lasts a moment anyway. After the fact, we often ask ourselves, "Is this what I broke my relationship with God for?" Submission is active and not passive. When my flesh is struggling, I must throw myself in God's direction. Disobedience defers the blessings of God. Anything I give power to has the power over me. Take your power back and you'll get your life back. Order follows obedience and obedience releases overflow! The word of God works if you work it!

Journey Note

83 *Today's Gem*

Your life is a game of connecting dots to God. I remember playing this game as a child and initially, the image didn't make sense. However, as more dots became connected, the picture became perfect. Know this, sis, God has a plan for your life and you need to trust Him daily. If you don't, you'll waste time being frustrated by your own past or trying to figure out your future. When God gets through with us, what looked like an image that didn't make sense will be a picture-perfect image of Him.

Journey Note

84 *Today's Gem*

We must do the work. A friend shared recently that we must understand that the only way for ungodly behavior to loose its grip on our lives, is for us to memorize, commit our lives to, and gain an understanding of the principles of the Word of God. Hebrews 4:12 says, "For the Word of God is quick, powerful, and full of life; sharper than the sharpest dagger; it penetrates deeply, even to the dividing of soul from spirit; yes, to the inmost parts thereof. It is skilled in judging and sifts the purpose, intents, and thoughts of the heart!" The word of God works. Follow the instructions in Psalms 119:11: "Hide the word in your heart, so you won't sin against the Lord." Find a scripture, commit it to memory and watch it work wonders in your life. Remember, you must do the work.

Journey Note

85 Today's Gem

You were born to do the ridiculous. That means, you've been called to do what's never been done before. Don't worry about being equipped—for God promised to supply all our needs according to His riches in glory. When God calls ordinary people to do extraordinary work expect to be ridiculed. Remember Noah? God called Noah to build a boat in a place that had never experienced water. The people thought Noah was crazy for obeying God. In the end, Noah's obedience saved his life and it changed his life. Sis, what is God calling you to do that has never been done before?

Journey Note

86 *Today's Gem*

Whenever God calls you to do the ridiculous, revelation must be your reality. Every day you must ask, "What did God say to me today?" When revelation is your reality, you live your life according to the vision and not according to the visual. Habakkuk 2:3 states to write the vision and make it plain on tablets, that he may run who reads it. For the vision is yet for an appointed time—but at the end it will speak, and it will not lie. Write what God shows you so you won't be distracted and detoured by what you see. 2 Corinthians 5:7 reminds us to walk by faith and not by sight. God is faithful to perform what He promised…it's just a matter of time.

Journey Note

87 *Today's Gem*

The season of defeat is over in your life if you would just activate the word of God. The season of struggle is over in your life if you would just actualize the promises of God. If God said it, that settles it. God knows that. The devil knows that. Do you know that? God's will is stronger than any force on earth and His will is available to work in your life if you would just agree with God. The moment you agree with God's will for your life is the moment your life changes. Why? In this dimension of restoration, you can expect unexpected blessings.

Journey Note

88 *Today's Gem*

Make this your season to pursue purity. This can be your season to pursue purity in your thoughts, purity in your heart, purity in your relationships and purity in your walk with God. Purity is produced when you seek truth. Truth releases power, which is attached to purpose and provision. How? An empowered life means you are now equipped to tap into the omniscience, omnipotence and omnipresence of God. Release the presence of God in you to help you seek Him. Can you imagine what that meeting will be like? When you position yourself to meet God — He will greet Himself!

Journey Note

89 *Today's Gem*

There are no missed opportunities in God—only divine providence! You are where you're supposed to be when you're supposed to be there. The supernatural sequence of your life is perfect. Stop being driven by unresolved issues, unanswered questions and uncertainties that plague you. It's best to be led by God, not driven by other forces. No matter how long it takes, wait on the Lord, be of good courage and He will strengthen your heart. Girl, remember—your times are in His hands.

Journey Note

90 *Today's Gem*

Some pain can't be prayed away and it can't be taken away by the laying on of hands. For some pain, God has to reach into your place of pain and snatch it out. However, you have to be still long enough to allow God to do it. Staying busy, running from relationship from relationship, or ignoring the pain only numbs you temporarily. Eventually, the pain creeps back to the top and cripples you. Sis, you are entitled to be whole. Flip the script on your pain—be still and let God do it. Once you begin to heal, you'll realize that your pain has become the fuel that drives you back to your divine position—where's that? Walking and living as a woman of passion and purpose. Remember, God never wastes a hurt! 2 Corinthians 1:4 states, "God comforts us so that we can comfort others."

Journey Note

91 *Today's Gem*

God is turning your situation around. Even when you can't see God moving, He's working on your behalf. Stop being bound by your context and focus on your content. Don't see the obstacle—see God! The Bible declares in 1 John 4:4, "Greater is He that is in you than He that is in the world". If the greater one is in you, then your situation must change. If your turmoil is great, your peace will be greater. If your sickness is great, then your healing will be greater. If your bondage is great, then your freedom will be greater. If your brokenness is great, then your wholeness will be greater. Shift your thinking from great to greater because your content (Christ in you) is much greater than your context (what's happening around you).

Journey Note

92 *Today's Gem*

Psalms 61:1–4 says, "Hear my cry, O God; listen to my prayer. From the end of the earth I will cry to You, when my heart is overwhelmed and fainting; lead me to the rock that is higher than I (yes, a rock that is too high for me)." Many of us have felt overwhelmed by life's many light afflictions—especially when we try to "help God" resolve what we perceive to be negative circumstances. However, after having cried out to God in the midst of "fiery trials," I've discovered that God uses these times to increase my capacity to receive more of Him. *More of God means less of me!* With each life encounter I build God an altar and name it! My journey to the "high places" in God are full of lessons on trust, acceptance, security, peace, joy, love, long-suffering, compassion, obedience, kindness, gentleness, humility and maturity.

Journey Note

93 *Today's Gem*

Purity is a powerful witness! Don't let the devil fool you. Don't let what the media portrays fool you. Don't let your need to be affirmed, approved and accepted fool you. When you make a determination in your mind and a commitment in your heart to be faithful to God, you set in motion the divine providence and protection of God. A life of purity provokes a man to respect, honor and value you—even when he doesn't understand. In spite of how it feels, hold your ground and know that God is up to something on your behalf. When God says no—when God says don't—it's because He has something greater in mind for you. Keep standing, girl—rejection is God's protection on your life!

Journey Note

94 *Today's Gem*

In John 2:5, the mother of Jesus told the servants, "Whatever He says to you, do it." The servants took the water pots, filled them with water and at the wedding at Cana of Galilee, He turned the water into wine. Today, if you will begin to do whatever Jesus tells you to do, He will turn your water to wine. He will turn your misery to ministry; your frustration to freedom; your depression and discontent into destiny if you would only completely surrender everything to Him. Remember, sis, Jesus is Lord whether you declare it or not. Jesus is Lord whether you live it or not. Come out today. How? With your hands up!

Journey Note

95 *Today's Gem*

Why do some people never seem to grow in the Lord? Why can't others move into the fullness of purpose and destiny God has for them? I believe it's because we say "Yes, Lord" with our mouths, but our lives display "Not now, Lord." To completely surrender means dying to myself and to my desires. To live a "yes, Lord" means I will fast when I feel like eating. It means I will give when I would rather spend my money on myself. It means I will enter into praise and worship as my first reaction and not my last resort. The attitude of surrender means putting God first in all my ways, thoughts and words. Our acknowledgement of His Lordship determines the success and quality of our lives.

Journey Note

96 Today's Gem

Behind the passionate life of every passionate woman of God is a passion for God and His word. 2 Timothy 3:16–17 declares that "scripture is given by inspiration of God and is profitable for doctrine, reproof, correction, instruction in righteousness, that the woman of God may be complete, and thoroughly equipped for every good work." Through His word, God speaks straight from His heart to yours. God's word is the heart of God. It gives you strength, wisdom, guidance, joy and instruction. Psalms 34:8 invites you, O passionate woman of God, "to taste and see that the Lord is good."

Journey Note

97 Today's Gem

There is pleasure in doing things God's way. It's called the order of God. Order releases favor, abundance and wealth. Order releases promotion, promise and prosperity. Trust God and leave the details of your life in His hands. He has already worked it out and it's beyond what you imagine. Remember, He is able to exceed abundantly above all that we can ask or think according to the power that works in us. The moment you lose yourself in Christ, with all the pretense and pressure of trying to impress people—at that very moment—you'll find your true self. You are not forgotten—you are being preserved.

Journey Note

98 *Today's Gem*

Today is a good day. It's a good day to celebrate your strength. It's a good day to recognize that anything the devil sent your way to kill you no longer has power over you—because you're still here. It's a good day to square your shoulders, hold your head up high and stand up straight. You're not bent over anymore. You are more than loosed—you're free to take a step in the direction of your destiny. You're not just a leading lady; you're the producer of the show. Take your life back and get ready—for your best days are ahead of you. Ahead begins—*right now.*

Journey Note

99   *Today's Gem*

God has not forgotten you. He has not forsaken you. He forgives you—so forgive yourself. Stop rehearsing the past and determine in your mind to allow God to transform your pain into power. The Bible challenges us to lay aside every weight and the sin that so easily besets us. It's time for you to get yourself together and move on. God is in your future waiting on you to say *yes* to His will for your life. You didn't come this far for your life to end like this. Turn the page—it's the beginning of the next chapter and it's all good.

Journey Note

100 *Today's Gem*

God is always right! Always! His leadings are always consistent with His word. His direction for your life will always line up with who you were created to be. John 15:16 declares that "you did not choose me, but I chose you and appointed you that you should go and bear fruit, and that your fruit should remain." Stay in your lane and measure up to God's plan for you life.

Journey Note

101 *Today's Gem*

Faith is the substance of things hoped for, the evidence of things not seen. Without faith, it is impossible to please God. Thus, ladies, your hope cannot be put in some dreamed-up future or fantasy. It must be in the God who knows your past, present and future. It must be in the God who loves you enough to give you the best. Elisabeth Elliott said, "Faith does not eliminate questions. But faith knows where to take them." A woman of faith does not numb her longings and desires. Instead, she embraces God so tightly that she faces her waiting period with peace, not bitterness. If you work…God will wait. If you wait…God will work.

Journey Note

102 Today's Gem

Psalms 139:14 reminds us "to praise God, for we are fearfully and wonderfully made; marvelous are your works God; and that my soul knows very well." It follows then that, that if I'm a work of art created by God, I'm marvelous and so are you! Bishop Jakes wrote in *Sacred Promises For God's Woman*, "When you lack belief in yourself, you lack belief in God." You are perfect in the eyes of He who made you. As the master composer, His song of "you" would not be anything less than brilliant. Recognize His handiwork and celebrate the incredible masterpiece of you!

Journey Note

103 *Today's Gem*

Proverbs 3:5 (AMP) declares, "Lean on, trust in, and be confident in the Lord with all your heart and mind and do not rely on your own insight or understanding." Verse 6 continues with, " In all your ways know, recognize, and acknowledge Him, and He will direct and make straight and plain your paths." For many, God is training us to trust Him. How? With His silence. We don't like unanswered questions or answers that are different from our expectations. God won't tell you what you don't need to know yet, sis. Instead, obey the last instruction He gave you—for your obedience breaks the silence of God.

Journey Note

104 *Today's Gem*

Don't panic, sis—God's got you. Trust Him to perfect all that concerns you—the bills, the children, your job, your marriage, your singleness, your ministry, your emotions, your desires. God is growing you. He is expanding your capacity to receive more of Him. The fire of God is to prove you, to purify you, and to perfect you. Psalms 66:12 (AMP) says that "after you come through—not over, not under, not around, but through the fire—God will bring you into a place of abundance and refreshing." The trying of your faith worketh patience and proves to God that He can trust you with trouble and triumph.

Journey Note

105 *Today's Gem*

Philippians 2:13 says, "For it is God who is effectually at work in you, energizing and creating in you the power and desire, both to will and to work for His good pleasure and satisfaction and delight." God is more concerned with your ultimate destiny than your immediate comfort. Your process is an indication of your destiny. Whatever God is working out of you is so that He can purify it for His glory. You already have all that you need to be effective for Christ. You are a power-packed, purpose-driven Princess in the Kingdom of God. Now walk, talk and live like you know it—the devil does.

Journey Note

Purity comes at a high price. God seeks to purify us and all that we say we love…whether it be friendship, a spiritual blessing, a romantic interest, an intent or desire of the heart—it must be purified. How? You must pour it out before the Lord to be tried in the fire of God—just as a silversmith refines silver. This test of purity is to prove whether you love the Lord your God with all your heart and soul. Give it, or them, to God. It's simply a determination of the mind. The fire takes away the impurities—whatever survives the fire of God reflects Him and is given back to you.

Journey Note

107 Today's Gem

Can you lay down everything for the love of God? Jesus said in Luke 22:42, "Not my will, but always Yours be done." He made a choice to be crucified. Addison Leitch said, "When the will of God crosses the will of man, somebody has to die." To be crucified with Christ is to live, sis! How? Once you allow God to have your fear, doubt, insecurity, low self-esteem, unbelief, unholy appetites, neediness for attention, adoration and affection, and nail them to the cross, all that's left is Christ. Can you imagine your life without all that *self-imposed* drama? Now that's a reflection of peace that surpasses all understanding.

Journey Note

108 *Today's Gem*

Sis, God wants to make you a tree. Okay, like a tree...
You know — that tree in Psalms 1:3 planted by the
water, ready to bring forth fruit in its season. But first,
you must endure some seasons that will appear to be
to your detriment. You go through the Fall changing
into many glorious colors in preparation for the cold,
lonely and barren times of the winter — or so it seems.
You see, when you can't see God moving, you must
know that He's working. Spring comes and with it
comes new life, new splendor, new blossoms and new
beauty. No matter where you are in the seasons of life,
always remember that God is in full control.

Journey Note

109 Today's Gem

Rainbows are God's evidence of promise. However, a rainbow is created from a mixture of sun and rain. In other words, joy and pain produce promise. Let me say that another way—the Son (Jesus) and the rain (your suffering) produce promise, too. It's called process. When process and promise meet—it's your hour to shine—it's called purpose. So be not weary in well doing, for in due season, not only will you reap, but God will turn your world from gray—into a radiance of color!

Journey Note

110 Today's Gem

Talk to God about it. Not your girlfriend, not your co-worker—not even your prayer partner. Talk to God about it. Often, silence denotes discipline, patience and trust in God. David said in Psalms, "Truly my heart waits silently for God." David said in Psalm 23, "He leads me beside still and quiet waters." It is there—in the quietness that God refreshes and restores our soul. Waiting silently is very hard to do—but it is possible. Today, God is asking you to try Him—you've tried everything and everybody else and you're still waiting. Now, wait on the Lord, be of good courage and He will strengthen, fortify and encourage your heart.

Journey Note

111 *Today's Gem*

When you don't have enough, give it to Jesus! I'm talking about everything from not having enough money to not having enough compassion. I'm talking about not having enough peace to not having enough joy. I'm, talking about not having enough love coming in and enough love flowing out. In Matthew 14, Jesus took two fish and five loaves of bread: He took it, blessed it, broke it and gave it. God took "not enough" and it became so much that there were leftovers. In the words of Ruth Stall, "If my life is broken when given to Jesus, it is because pieces will feed a multitude, while a loaf will satisfy only one." Give what you have left to God, sis—your heart, your energy, your money, your desires, your dreams, your goals, your love, your whatever. He will take your "not enough" and make it who He is—Elohim—the God of "more than enough!"

Journey Note

112 *Today's Gem*

Celebrate transition! God is nudging you to shift. Transition is not comfortable because as soon as you become familiar with where you are, it's time to move again. The place of transition is also the "place of refining." In this place, you encounter the fire of God. The fire of God consumes everything except your desire to know Him! In the fire of God you get revelation! In the fire of God you get inspiration! In the fire of God you get transformation! In the fire of God you get direction! So, yes, celebrate transition because transition is your friend. It comes to move you from what has been to what is coming!

Journey Note

113 *Today's Gem*

The Bible says in Psalms 37:4, "Delight yourself also in the Lord, and He will give you the desires and secret petitions of your heart." God is not looking for a part-time delight. He wants you to take pleasure in His presence. He wants your soul—the seat of your emotions—to be satisfied after each and every encounter with Him! God wants you to get so entrenched in Him that not even *you* can tell where you end and He begins. Once you and God reach this place, the desires of your heart will begin to manifest because now your heart beats in sync with His! You love what God loves. You hate what He hates. You feel what He feels. Now, you can't be denied, because God cannot—He will not—deny Himself!

Journey Note

114 Today's Gem

God made us who we are. Ephesians 2:10 says, "For we are God's handiwork, recreated in Christ Jesus, that we may do those good works which God planned in advance that we should walk in them." You are unique. You are priceless — so valuable that your worth is limitless! Only you can fulfill the purpose for which you were created. So, never give up being who you are in an attempt to "be like someone else." You are no more than or less than anyone else — just different. If God had not made you as He did, you wouldn't be able to persevere as you have. *And sometimes*, you've just got to remind yourself!

Journey Note

115 Today's Gem

Hey, woman—do you realize how intensely God loves you? When God says *no*, that doesn't mean you're not loved. Think back. Hasn't He blessed you? Hasn't He held you through some rough places? He's still holding you! If He doesn't cater to you and your self-absorbed requests, it's love. When God says no, it's because He knows you may get what you want—but you might not want what you get! Woman, God loves you. He's crazy about you! You are the apple of His eye. Max Lucado said, "If God had a wallet, your picture would be in it. He sends you flowers every spring and listens every time you talk." He's tugging at your heart right now. It's okay—feel the love.

Journey Note

116 *Today's Gem*

Are you experiencing lack in your life? Then maybe you need to reevaluate your giving. 2 Corinthians 9:6–10 says, "He who sows sparingly will reap sparingly and he who sows generously will reap generously and with blessings." Let each woman give as she has made up her mind, not reluctantly, for God loves a cheerful giver and He is able to make every favor blessing come to you in abundance so that you may always possess enough. God provides seed to the sower and will provide and multiply your resources for sowing. Your seed is anything that can multiply: love, time, money or kindness, and your harvest is what comes back to you, like joy, relationships or finances. If you don't have enough to be a harvest, use it as seed and allow God to multiply it. Try outgiving God! You'll love the results.

Journey Note

117 *Today's Gem*

I want to remind you again of 1 John 3:1 — "See, what an incredible quality of love the Father has given us, that we should be called the children of God." God's love for us doesn't depend on what we say, what we do, on our looks or intelligence, on our success or popularity, on our choices or our performance. God's love for us is not based on events or circumstances. God doesn't say I love you *if*…His love is unconditional. To love without condition is not to love without concern. Don't confuse unconditional love with unconditional approval. God doesn't approve of betrayal, selfishness, pride or disobedience. God's love continues even when we blow it! His love is His magnet. Jeremiah 31:3 says, "I have loved you with an everlasting love; therefore with loving kindness have I drawn you!" Girl, it never stops!

Journey Note

118 *Today's Gem*

God is bringing the high places down. But you must do your part. Okay—it happened. Whatever that is! 1 John 1:9 says, "If we freely admit that we have sinned and confess our sins, He is faithful and just to forgive our sins and cleanse us from all unrighteousness"—that is, everything not in conformity to His will and purpose, thought and action. Get up, get over it and get going. Ask God to help you work on the weakness that weakens you. When you change, everything changes. Submit your brokenness to God. In your weakness, He is made stronger in you. You don't have to be afraid of success, for in Christ you can handle it. Are you afraid right now? It's okay—do it anyway. For the truth is, if it doesn't require faith, it doesn't please God. Take every step—not by what you see but by what you know God sees for you.

Journey Note

119 *Today's Gem*

Whatever takes God's place in your life is an idol. Whether it's a job, a relationship, a ministry, a material possession or a lifestyle—if it's first in your life, it has taken God's place. Only you know in your heart who or what has that #1 spot. When God tells you to let someone go but you hold on to them, it's idolatry. Yes, it's going to be painful because it won't feel good. It takes real trust to know that you can give up what you have and get back something better. God wants to wean you from the lesser and give you the greater. God's plans for your life are so much better than yours. Whatever it costs you, sis, it's worth the pain, discomfort and risk to make the switch. Is He talking to you? Only you know that!

Journey Note

120 *Today's Gem*

Matthew 23:11 says, "But the greatest among you shall be your servant." Nobody is too great to help others. Touch somebody's life today who can't return the gesture. Love people—not crowds. Seek solutions—not credit. Lift somebody else's spirit—not put them down to make yourself look better. Listen, insecure people project an image of who they want to be. It's a miserable way to live and a facade that's impossible to maintain. The root of insecurity is really the fear of rejection. But when you are meek, humble and lowly in spirit—meaning you project Christ, not self—you're already grounded in love and have nothing to lose... *everything to gain!*

Journey Note

1 23 Today's Gem

We must learn to love mercy. We must become a place of refuge for one another. Become a safe place for your sister. Become a place of healing for another woman. Resist the opportunity to wound another woman. Break down the walls that provoke us to tear each other down. We must love mercy. Tap into the oil of your past experiences, past pain, and become a source of refreshing. Today, turn your misery into ministry, for when you take care of God's business He is faithful and just to take care of yours.

Journey Note

124 Today's Gem

Did you know that a mirror has two faces? The first face is the real you. The second face is the you with all the makeup, touch-ups and cover-ups. But today, the question is—who do you resemble? It doesn't matter which face you're checking because at some point in your walk with Christ, you ought to look like Christ. 2 Corinthians 3:16–18 says, "Whenever a person turns to the Lord in repentance, the veil is stripped off and taken away. Where the Spirit of the Lord is there is liberty. Now with an unveiled face, the more you read the word, the more you are transformed and transfigured into His very own image in ever increasing splendor." Be the image—it's eternal.

Journey Note

125 *Today's Gem*

Did you know that you are God's choice? God called you to do a specific work — no more, no less. So what are you waiting for? Are you waiting on people to affirm you? Are you stuck in the place of your last mistake? Are you still struggling with habits that God has already given you victory over? Girl, there is a place in God beyond average. There is a place in God that surpasses "this is how I am." There is a place in God that extends past "I'm doing the best that I can." How do you get there? *You* must do the work. Read your word, communicate with God, establish an intimate relationship with God. Listen, when you are God's choice, nothing else matters.

Journey Note

1 26 Today's Gem

God wants us to want Him. When we realize that it's Him we want, we become free to identify the longings, loneliness and emptiness inside as our signal that we need to draw closer to God. With open arms, we need to ask God to fill us with more of Himself. Psalms 62:1 says, "For God alone my soul waits in silence." Stop availing yourself to illusions and fantasies created by living in denial. Stop managing the matters of your heart with your emotions. Respond to those cravings from your spirit as it is submitted to the Spirit of God. Galatians 5:16 says, "Walk in the Spirit and it is impossible to do what you want to do!"

Journey Note

1 27 Today's Gem

God is an awesome God. If you are in Him and He is in you…guess what? You are awesome, too! Too many of us base our personal worth on what we believe the most important people in our lives think about us. We are constantly looking for someone else to tell us we are significant. Your value is not based on what somebody else thinks about you. Ephesians 2:10 says, "We are His workmanship, created in Christ Jesus to do good works, which God prepared in advance for us to do." When your view of God changes, your view of yourself will change, too. Once you begin to talk right about God, you'll talk right about yourself, too!

Journey Note

128 Today's Gem

Have you taken ownership of what doesn't belong to you? Well, you cannot consecrate what is not yours! It's not your gift. It's not your ministry. The Lord doesn't want you to present your plans or your agenda to Him. He wants you to present your body. Oswald Chambers said, "There is only one thing you can consecrate to God and that is your right to yourself. If you give God your right to yourself, He will make a holy experiment out of you. His experiments always succeed." Today, I challenge you to a reckless abandonment to Jesus Christ. The result—you'll become a wellspring of originality as Christ works through you.

Journey Note

129 Today's Gem

Make your habitation in Christ. The Bible says in Psalms 16:11, "You will show me the path of life; in your presence is fullness of joy, at your right hand there are pleasures forevermore." In His presence there is also common sense, discipline, consistency, humility, love, peace, gentleness, goodness and meekness. In His presence the renewing of your mind takes place so that you can discern the will of God for your life. Outside His presence, your convictions make you a self-righteous fanatic. But there is something amazingly humbling about being submitted, devoted, and loyal to God. You become *his* woman!

Journey Note

130 *Today's Gem*

God wants to fill us with Himself. Why? Because your unmet needs make you a slave to others. Ephesians 3:18–20 (AMP) says, "that you may have the power to apprehend and grasp with all the saints the experience of that love what is the breadth, length, height and depth of God's love. That you may really come to know through experience for yourself the love of Christ which far surpasses mere knowledge; that you may be filled (through all your being) with the fullness of God and become a body completely full of and flooded by God Himself." Now He can do above and beyond your highest hopes, dreams, and thoughts. Philippians 4:19 says, "God wants to and will liberally supply your every need." Be who God made you. He's satisfied—you should be, too.

Journey Note

131 *Today's Gem*

Matthew 24:6 declares, "And ye shall hear of wars and rumors of wars: see that ye be not troubled: for all these things must come to pass, but the end is not yet." Take comfort, refuge, and find peace today in Christ. Peace is not the absence of turmoil—it is the equalizer of God in the midst of turmoil that causes us to rest. John 16:33 says "In Christ ye shall have peace." Philippians 4:7 declares, "And the peace of God shall keep your hearts and minds through Jesus Christ." The safest place, woman of God, in the midst of all that is happening today, Psalms 91:1 says, is "The secret place of the Most High God." Here, His angels have charge over you to accompany you, defend and preserve you in all your ways.

Journey Note

132 Today's Gem

Matthew 6:12 states, "And forgive us our debts, as we also have forgiven and have given up resentment against our debtors". In other words, God, treat me like I treat others. God extend to me the mercy that I have extended to others. God, love on me the way I love others. God, please bless me the way I bless others — *do we really want God to do that?* If that were the measuring stick of God's release in your life, what would be coming your way right now? Examine your heart. Analyze the purity of your thoughts toward others. Do we really want God to remember as long as we do? We've got work to do — let's get busy!

Journey Note

133 Today's Gem

God is calling us as women back to our place of femininity. Inside each of us is the fragrance of a rose, the softness of silk and the beauty of satin. Inside us is the power to become who we really are. God wants us to live fruitful lives, therefore we must live a life of purity. Purity in our hearts, purity in our minds, purity in our spirits—purity in our femininity. The book of Psalms 19:12 declares, "Cleanse me from my secret faults." It's not the big things or the obvious things that challenge us—therefore, ask the Lord to prepare you, preserve you, prove you. He wants you to be His woman—God's woman.

Journey Note

134 Today's Gem

Get up and get going! Decide to live a life that pleases God in all respects. Set your heart's desire on giving God glory with your lifestyle—not just your lips. When the Spirit of the Lord prompts you to do something, respond to it—don't reject it. Seek to obey God on a moment-by-moment basis. God wants all of you all the time—not just on Sunday morning. In order to be full of God, you must first empty out old ways, old habits and old thought patterns. You can do it! Yes, you can! God said so! Remember, He can't lie!

Journey Note

135 Today's Gem

God wants to form Himself in you. Yes, He wants your whole heart. But He also wants to give you His heart. Then, you'll love like He loves; you'll speak the truth as He would; you'll extend compassion—even to those you feel deserve your wrath. Jesus wants to make you full of Himself. God wants you to experience the liberty of real love—God love—agape (unconditional love). Can't you hear Him calling you? Yes, *you!* Jesus longs to entertain you in His secret place—for in this place you will take off religion and put on relationship.

Journey Note

GEMS
for the
SOUL

136 *Today's Gem*

Ladies, ladies, ladies! I feel the need to remind you that we as women cannot separate our emotions from our physical state. The person who touches your body in an intimate and sexual way, also touches your emotions. You cannot have sex with a person and remain emotionally untouched no matter how hard you try. You cannot give your body without giving your heart. This is not a sin issue as much as it is a heart issue. This is not about you falling, as much as it is about your lack of ruling and reigning in every area of your life. Yes, you're wounded, yes, you're hurting, yes, you're broken, yes, you're bleeding—but that is not an excuse to allow your choices to separate you from God. Now more than ever, you must press your way into His presence. If you let Him, He will make you whole.

Journey Note

137 *Today's Gem*

We are at war! It may be a war of words, a war of emotions, a war of rumors or a war of the mind! Whatever it is, don't be afraid because God is there—He is a very present help in your time of trouble. Rest in the Lord and wait patiently for Him. Be comforted today, for *your* warfare has ended! 2 Chronicles 20 says, "Be not afraid or dismayed at this onslaught for the battle is not yours, but God's." Verse 17 says, "There is no need to fight in this battle. Just take your position, square your shoulders, hold your head up, stand still and watch God." We are empowered to prosper and be victorious in the face of the enemy because the covenant on my life is greater than the attack on my life.

Journey Note

138 *Today's Gem*

You are an example of God's intent to change the world! You have value! You have worth! You have purpose! God has need of you—that's why you are here! God wants to release you from that spirit of rejection! Okay, so maybe your mother didn't want you and all your life you've been called a "mistake" so that's how you live your life—as if it's a mistake. Well, from God's heart to yours, Jeremiah 1:5 says, "Before I formed you in the womb, I knew you and approved you, set you apart, and consecrated you." Psalms 139:17 states, "The Lord's thoughts toward you are precious!" He wants you to know right now—you've been rejected to rule and reign with Him. Now, Queen, take your throne.

Journey Note

139 *Today's Gem*

The spirit of offense is running rampant in the Body of Christ. This spirit doesn't come alone, either. With offense comes unresolved anger. With unresolved anger comes bitterness. With bitterness comes resentment. With resentment comes rage. With rage comes vindication and ultimately believers find themselves stuck in a pit of unforgiveness. What's going on in you? Why are you allowing an old offense and an old offender to control your life? Unforgiveness pushes you to compromise what you know is right. Today, God wants to give you grace for purpose. He wants to empower you to release what you've been holding on to. He wants to give you grace to see yourself as the "victor" and not the "victim" any longer! In the words of Maya Angelou, "You may be changed by what happens to you; but you can refuse to be reduced by it!"

Journey Note

140 *Today's Gem*

Pain often drives people to act in ways that are comforting and anesthetizing in the short term, but negative and damaging in the long term. Often, overwhelming circumstances come to shift us into the next stage of purpose. God can and does bring purpose to pain in the lives of His children. However, He does not comfort us to make us comfortable. He comforts us to make us comforters. God wants you to realize today that you cannot be anything else to your family and friends until you become what you are supposed to be to Him. God wants to speak a word to you in the midst of your trauma. It's never too late to begin again with God. You did not come this far for your story to end like this…get up and get moving—God has plans for you!

Journey Note

141 Today's Gem

Don't let people disturb your peace! Others will attempt to steal your peace because they don't have any. You've heard it before—misery loves company. Guess what? Peace loves company, too. Surround yourself with people and things that contribute to your peace. Determine to have peaceful conversations. Peace is a promise from God to you if you keep your mind stayed on him.

Journey Note

142 Today's Gem

There is a "little girl" in all of us. We all want affirmation, approval, adoration and acceptance. We all want to be the apple of someone's eye. Too often, we as women continually nurse frailties that zap our energy, our confidence and our self-esteem. What we should be doing is nurturing our gifts, our value and our self-worth. In the words of the gospel group Mary Mary, God already has made you beautiful. Girl, you are just the way God intended you to be—unique! So, from today forward, when you look in the mirror—say, "I love me with all my flaws and downfalls." Just be your best (no, not for "them"), cause to Him (no, not your man), in Him in Christ, you *already* are the best! *You go, girl.*

Journey Note

143 *Today's Gem*

Hello there, woman of God. Great woman of God! No, you don't have ordination papers or a missionary license, but you have been called to the Kingdom for such a time as this. You do have a Kingdom assignment. But to be effective, you must take risks and accept change. Grow through challenges—be totally honest with yourself first. Then, and only then, can you be honest with others. Correct erroneous beliefs and assumptions for they limit your potential. Respect your vulnerabilities. Know what you like, so if necessary, you know when to run. Heal old wounds and refuse to accept new ones. Wave goodbye to guilt—for if the devil can keep you guilty, he can keep you defeated. Treat yourself with respect and teach others to do the same. Sista girl, fill you cup first, then nourish others from the overflow. Take ownership of your own excellence and know that Philippians 1:6 is true: "He that hath begun a good work in you, will perform it until the day of Jesus Christ."

Journey Note

144 *Today's Gem*

Deception lies in the hearts of those who think reality has nothing to offer. You live in an illusion. Consequently, you live your life full of anger, bitterness, resentment, resistance, jealousy and sadness because these emotions are easier than the grief you would have to endure if you took your situation off life support. Yes, it's alive—but there is no life. Yes, it's functioning, but it's mechanical—it's the same motion over and over again. Denial exempts you from being healed. Come on, open your eyes and see it for what it is. Let God deal with the pain of your situation so that you can walk in the power of your resurrected dreams.

Journey Note

145 Today's Gem

I am a woman. I am God's woman. I am a woman walking in total confidence of God to the praise of His glory. I am a VIP! I have Value in Christ, I have Identity in Christ and I have Purpose in Christ. This status is not about what I have—it's about where I am. Ephesians 1:11 states that "In Him also, we have obtained an inheritance. I am sealed with the Holy Spirit of promise, and In Him, I have the assurance that the Holy Spirit is the guarantee of my inheritance." Get ready for what's coming—resurrection, restoration and restitution!

Journey Note

146 *Today's Gem*

Women who love obsessively are full of fear. They fear being alone, being unlovable and unworthy, being abandoned, ignored or destroyed. Consequently, they give—what they call love—in the desperate hope that the object of their affection will take care of their fears. Instead, the fears and obsessions become worse until giving love in order to get it back becomes a driving force in their life. When that doesn't work, they love even harder and it becomes a cycle of destruction, devastation, and disappointment. Is this you? If so, God wants you to stop measuring the degree of your love by the depth of your torment. That's not love—that's obsession. But the good news is this—Jesus is waiting to cover you with the healing that is in His wings.

Journey Note

147 Today's Gem

Are you a woman with healthy self-esteem? If so, then you accept yourself fully, even in the midst of becoming better. You accept others as they are without trying to change them to meet your needs. When you are a fulfilled woman, you find validation in God, rather than searching for that sense of self-worth in an earthly relationship. You don't need to be needed in order to feel worthy, and you do not expose yourself to the exploitation of those who are not interested in your well-being. A woman with healthy sense of self is secure in knowing that God's love never fails, never ends, never changes.

Journey Note

148 Today's Gem

Sis, stop running around looking for love. The only reason we as women do that is because we have not fully embraced how intensely God loves us. God is a personal God and He is deeply committed to loving each of us. He made that decision long before we failed—so repent for rejecting His love. Repent for allowing guilt to stay longer than it was supposed to. Guilt insults God's mercy. Open your heart, unzip you spirit and hear God calling you in the midst of the very thing you're trying to run from. Stand still and know the *nothing* you can do can make God change his mind about you.

Journey Note

149 *Today's Gem*

So you say you want to know what love is? Well God wants to show you. I Corinthians 13 says that love endures long. Love is patient and kind. It's not envious, jealous, or haughty. Love is not conceited, arrogant rude, or inflated with pride. Love gives and gives and gives—until you are consumed and compelled to submit to its authority! Love is not self-seeking or resentful. Love bears up under anything and everything that comes. Love endures without weakening. Love *never* fails. Now, in order to detect the counterfeit, you must have a thorough understanding of the real thing. Is it love? Compare what you see, hear and perceive to God's definition. Then, you decide.

Journey Note

150 *Today's Gem*

It's time to take off the mask! It's time to stop pretending like we are superwoman—no problems, no struggles, no pain, no skeletons, no past! Who is the real you? Do you like her? Do you know her? Have you seen her lately? Can you look in the mirror and say "I love you"? God's desire is that you increase. Ephesians 5:17 tells us to "firmly grasp what you know to be the will of God for your life—cling to it." The way you see yourself "in Christ" sets the boundary for increase in your life. Stop looking at what you are not, what you don't have, and begin to appreciate who you are. Stop dwelling on your failures long enough to catch a glimpse of the possibilities God is revealing. You determine how high you go in God.

Journey Note

151 Today's Gem

God wants to speak of hope and healing today. Specifically to you who have experienced the loss of a child through the tragedy of abortion. The foundation of hope, amid any human dilemma or human disobedience, will always be drawn from God's Word, not human reasoning. If you have ever made the decision to abort a child, Christ's death for our sins is complete payment for that choice, and complete forgiveness is available to you today. God's provisions for our past are sufficient and His promise for our future is incredibly bright. Your child is sitting in the presence of God. What an awesome motivation to live holy so that you can see them again. If comfort is what you need, then receive the peace of God in your heart right now.

Journey Note

152 Today's Gem

God is calling you to confront any feelings of guilt right now. Put guilt in its place. God wants you to deal with guilt head-on so that you might gain freedom from it. Don't allow the enemy to prey on your vulnerability and your pain. Rest your guilt-driven grief on God's grace. Refuse to allow it to regain any place in tormenting your mind or you feelings. There is no decision or choice that you can make that is powerful enough to keep you from the cleansing power of God's grace in Christ Jesus. Don't carry you pain away from Jesus— bring it to Him for His strength is perfect when our strength is gone.

Journey Note

153 Today's Gem

It's time for confrontation and this conflict is worth the risk. It's time for the new you to confront the old you. You're not that woman anymore! You're not shattered, aching, browbeaten or oppressed anymore! You are God's woman! You are every woman! You are who you need to be when you need to be it to the glory of God. You are intelligent and capable! You are phenomenal and you are supposed to be here. Your mistakes did not delete your destiny. You have been empowered by God to live beyond your circumstances. What God has spoken over your life will come to pass. Confrontation brings closure. Close the door and walk away from the darkness of your past—turn the key and unlock the door to your bright future!

Journey Note

154 *Today's Gem*

Today is "love on yourself" day! Women are nurturers by nature! We get so busy giving to others that we often neglect ourselves. Make an appointment to pamper yourself! Have a heart-to-heart with another sister you haven't spoken to in a while. Look in the mirror and speak words of life to yourself! Declare that today is the first day of the best days of your life. You are loveable. You are full of compassion and gifted with passion. You are accepted in the beloved and you have value! One last thing, at some point today, wrap your arms around your shoulders and give yourself a hug. "I love you"—that's from Christ *in* you—the hope of glory!

Journey Note

155 Today's Gem

To look at you is to see a woman who is independent enough to overcome any obstacles that stand between her and a goal, yet sensitive enough to be open-minded and caring. To look at you is to see a woman who knows when her help is needed and when it's better to let others figure things out for themselves. You have patience born of compassion, strength born of determination and caring born of real love. To look at you is to see a woman who's faced challenges and always survived. You are a woman who is respected and admired, and a reflection of God's grace and glory in the earth. You are a woman who is loved!

Journey Note

156 Today's Gem

Hungry people make poor grocery shoppers because they make impulsive decisions. Hunger has forced some to desperation and ultimately looking for food in places full of disease, waste and pestilence. Women who are hungry for love likewise make bad choices. Your deepest need for attention and emotional security can only be met through an intimate relationship with Jesus Christ. He wants to restore your soul. Jesus wants to heal that "little girl" in you that is longing to be loved! You don't have to perform for His love! You don't have to compromise for His love! You can't win His love. Like the woman at the well, you've been looking for love in all the wrong places…*Jesus* is waiting to give you what you need.

Journey Note

157 *Today's Gem*

Grief has many faces. Whether it's divorce, the loss of a job, a home, friends, our health, our dreams, or even our sense of who we are, grief is a part of life. It's also painful and as unique as the individual who has experienced the loss. The healing process is at best chaotic. You go back and forth through phases. From shock to denial to anger, to sadness to depression and finally into acceptance. It's not a matter of getting over it, but of integrating the loss into who you are and into who you must now become. Hebrews 4:15–16 says, "For we have not an high priest which cannot be touched with the feeling of our infirmities; but was in all points tempted like as we are, yet, without sin. Let us therefore come boldly into the throne of grace, that we may obtain mercy, and find grace to help in the time of need."

Journey Note

158 Today's Gem

Take a moment and reflect on what you have survived. Is it sexual abuse, rape, abortion, divorce, lesbianism, promiscuity, substance abuse, poverty, depression, confusion or betrayal? It's not important "what" it was. What is important is that you are still here. The place where the devil thought he destroyed you is the place where God starts to use you. Stop hiding behind the shame of your past. Stop allowing the enemy to cripple you with fear of others finding out what you used to do—that is *not* who you are. You are the righteousness of God! You are the praise of His glory! You are a joint heir with Christ! That place of pain has produced power. You are a vessel of honor with a lamp inside. What you survived was the process God used to crack you open for His glory to be revealed! Tell your story so that God can get the glory! Do you want to see God today? *Look in the mirror!*

Journey Note

159 Today's Gem

Today is a good day to celebrate! It's a good day to celebrate your strength. It's a good day to recognize that anything the devil sent your way to kill you no longer has power over you—because you are still here. It's a good day to square your shoulders, hold your head up high and stand up straight. You're not bent over anymore! Whose report will you believe? It doesn't matter what "they" say! God says you are more than a conqueror! That means for every struggle in your life, God has developed something in your character. You haven't made it this far for it to end like this. Don't let Destiny's Child celebrate alone—grab hold of faith and celebrate your survival!

Journey Note

160 Today's Gem

What's in your box? Your alabaster box. What has you so tied to yesterday that you can't perceive your future? Is it guilt over an abortion you had? Or maybe it's an extramarital affair that you can't seem to end because you've convinced yourself that you can't live without it. Is it bitterness from an old boyfriend that has caused you to turn to other women? Or maybe it's an addiction to alcohol or drugs that still torments you. Is it the fear of being alone that causes you to endure abuse in a relationship? I have a message for you from our Father—break open that box today and pour out the contents at His feet. Holy is your status, even when it's not your behavior. His love is waiting to heal you, to give you hope, to make you whole.

Journey Note

161 Today's Gem

The song says I'm every woman—it's all in me. Well, just what is it that's in you? Is it disobedience? Is it lust? Is it jealousy? Is it anger? Is it unforgiveness? Is it bitterness? Is it regret? If any of these or other ungodly traits occupy space in your life, then it's time for them to be evicted. God wants to replace your bitterness with compassion; your lust with self-control. God wants to replace your unforgiveness with forgiveness; your jealousy with contentment; and your regret with hope. Colossians 2:10 tells us that we are complete in Christ Jesus. So today, purpose in your heart to become all that God says you are. Kick the devil out of that space that belongs to God. The devil has taken residence *simply* because you have not commanded him to leave! Let today be the first day of a new you!

Journey Note

162 *Today's Gem*

Are you addicted to your story? Do you relive your pain over and over again so that you can be reinfected with your guilt, shame and humiliation? God had thrown those things into the sea of forgetfulness. Why do you continue to go fishing? God picks you up and carries you forward, and as soon as He puts you down for you to walk, you turn and run backward, afraid of what lies ahead. Sis, the worst is over now and what lies ahead is gonna bless your socks off. Don't worry about how God is going to do it—just know He plans to prosper you and not harm you.

Journey Note

163 *Today's Gem*

Your soul never gets saved. Renewal comes by way of your spirit being in control. We are in a season where women are in a battle between "the head" and "the heart." We are in a season where our "emotions" battle "our spirit." An appropriate response to this struggle is that when you sense a lack in what you feel, you must will an increase in your knowing. Even when you don't feel saved, you must rely on what you know. To be saved means you are by faith set free, healed and delivered! Now settle yourself, be still and *know!*

Journey Note

164 Today's Gem

The spirit of discouragement is running rampant in the Body of Christ. Most of us are in a place where we love God more than we ever have. Yet, we feel further away from Him than ever. I submit to you today— don't be fooled by what you don't feel. Be persuaded and know that Philippians 1:6 is still true—if God started it, He will perform it. Discouragement is the war between where your spirit wants to go and your soul wants to stay. There's a stretching going on and you can't explain it. That's how you know it's Him. Know this, too—you are the redeemed of the Lord and after you come through this valley of emptiness, you will be full of Him!

Journey Note

165 *Today's Gem*

God created us for intimacy. Intimacy is the ability to be yourself with another person without fear of rejection or intimidation. Intimacy creates an atmosphere of honesty, purity and love. Intimacy is sweetness, tenderness, gentleness and security. Intimacy produces power, life, joy and fulfillment. Intimacy requires private moments that add to you, not take away from or drain you. True intimacy is passionate and unforgettable. God is calling us to intimacy with Him—for in this secret place with Him, you are fortified, you are fulfilled and you are faith-filled.

Journey Note

166 *Today's Gem*

Girl, haven't you had enough yet? No, you really haven't—that's why things haven't changed. When you have really had enough, things change. You change! God wants you to know that there is so much more He has for you. You'll never be free until you despise the shackles that have you bound. Anything you keep feeding grows. Yet, if you starve a thing it dies. Quit breastfeeding what God wants you to starve to death. Start feeding what needs to survive. Start acting like you know and believe that your future is potent and full of purpose. Get up and do something *different*—I promise, you'll get different results.

Journey Note

167 *Today's Gem*

Is anger controlling your life? It is if you spend more time frowning than smiling. Anger controls your life if the glass is always half-empty and not half-full. Anger rules your life if it's always "the other person's" fault. Anger tells you that no matter what is going right, focus on what's wrong. Anger is deceptive and causes you to focus on things that won't resolve your suffering. Proverbs 25:28 states, "He who has no rule over her own spirit is like a city that is broken down and without walls." Give your anger to God and leave it there. Trust Him to take the sting away, heal your hurt, heal your life, and heal your mind. Remember, sis, patience in one moment of anger will help you escape 100 days of sorrow.

Journey Note

168 *Today's Gem*

Are you off to see the wizard? Sis, wake up and live in the real world. This is not Oz and your name is not Judy Garland playing the role of Dorothy. Snap out of denial and face yourself—the good, the bad and the ugly. Desperate people do desperate things. Stop! Stand still! Surround yourself with wise women and listen for a change. If you knew better your life would be better. Any lack in your life is actually a call to worship the only essence that can fill that void anyway. Girl, get yourself together and move on—there is so much life ahead of you!

Journey Note

169 *Today's Gem*

Often, we get in trouble, end up in trauma, endure tribulation and trials because we want to help God do His job. Psalms 37:23 states, "The steps of a good man are ordered by the Lord." Therefore, you cannot map out your journey and tell God which way you are going. The Bible tells us in Galatians 6:9, "Do not be weary in well doing, for in due season you shall reap if you faint not." Listen, sis, accomplishment without achievement is empty—it takes time to achieve anything of lasting value.

Journey Note

170 *Today's Gem*

Pain and suffering quite frequently are the precursors to change if we respond with Godly wisdom and not human logic. Further, the person in crisis must be the one to implement change. God's grace is always sufficient to guide us through the transition. It's not always the devil that is the adversary. Sometimes we are our own worst enemy. Get out of your way! Get out of God's way! What's happening in your life *right now* is to shift you higher up the mountain. Remember, the higher you go, the greater the revelation. The greater the revelation in your life, the greater the refreshing of the Lord in your life. I see all of us in the future and I still say: *things are looking so much brighter!!!* It's not over until God says so.

Journey Note

171 Today's Gem

Are you sick and tired of being sick and tired? When you really get to this point, you'll change! When you get truly disgusted with the guilt of waking up in the wrong bed, you'll change. When you get tired of picking up the pieces of your heart *again,* you'll change. When your head keeps chasing your heart through the same game—just a different name—and you discover it's not them, it's me—you'll change. When Peter runs out of money to give you to pay Paul, and unnecessary debt is about to give you a nervous breakdown, you will change. Bishop Noel Jones said, "Sometimes you have to almost lose your mind to change your mind." Psalms 119:133 says, "Direct my steps by your word and let no iniquity have dominion over me." Get your life back!

Journey Note

172 Today's Gem

Hey, precious woman of God—you are worth more than a fortune. You are a gift. You are a work of art. One of my coworkers walks around reminding us that as women, we are the prize. A gift doesn't ask to be bought and given. A diamond doesn't flag you down as you admire it manipulating you into buying it. It just is. If you really want it, you do what you have to do to secure it. It's the same way with a man. Ladies, just be the prize that you are. Focus on you, your life, your family, your dreams and your goals. The aroma of your fragrance of virtue will attract what and who belongs in your life.

Journey Note

173 *Today's Gem*

Through the affairs of the heart, God uncovers our motives, true intentions and what's really going on inside us. We call it longing. Often, God responds to our longing with silence. In the meantime, and a lot of times, we fill in for God in an attempt to meet that need or needs. What do we create? A mess! Now God has our attention and will often ask, "Can you hear me now daughter?" Psalms 62:1 says, "For God alone my soul waits in silence; from Him comes my salvation. Verse 5 states, "My soul, wait only upon God and silently submit to Him; for my hope and expectation are from Him."

Journey Note

174 *Today's Gem*

You're not that woman anymore. You're not broken, bruised, battered, beat down or bent over anymore. You are not depressed, dejected, despondent or denied. You are not suicidal or sickly, and shame doesn't live here anymore. *Stop* giving the devil power, access and authority with your words and your thoughts. Flip the script right now and give God that same power, access and authority. Life is in your tongue. You are intelligent, capable and qualified. You are a phenomenal woman. You are every woman and you are supposed to be here. What God has spoken over your life will come to pass. Close the gateway to your past—it's over because God said so.

Journey Note

175 Today's Gem

Unbridled passion always soars out of control and becomes the devil's playground. Unchecked emotions are like a roller coaster. First, you stand in a long line to get on a ride that you scream to get off. The journey starts off slow and it's fun. Then you climb a steep hill—only to suddenly drop at a speed that's dangerously fast. Then comes a turn here, a turn there and you're at the mercy of the ride. Now you're screaming, *"Let me off*!"* The truth is, sis, in the beginning you had a choice…you didn't have to ride. Guess what? You don't have to ride the emotional coaster you're on now, either. Get off! Stop chasing drama. Seek your thrills in a safe place—smack dab in the middle of God's will for *your* life!

Journey Note

176 *Today's Gem*

Drama is the result of unruly affections and out-of-control emotions. Ladies, drama does not denote passion. Drama is draining and zaps your energy and everybody that's attached to you. The love, attention, affirmation and security that you seek is waiting for you—minus the drama. Settle yourself! Christ in you, the hope of glory, wants to empower you to check yourself. Allow His word to transform your thinking, which will transform your life. Today, Jesus speaks peace to your private storms. Jesus wants to anchor your heart in Him! For only in Him, sis, can true joy, fulfillment and wholeness be found. Matthew 6:21 declares, "For where your heart is, there your treasure is also!" Where is your heart?

Journey Note

177 Today's Gem

You need to deal with unresolved issues! Why? Because in the daily devotional, *Word For You Today*, writer Bob Gass said, "If you don't submit your injury to the healing hand of God, today's wound becomes tomorrow's infection!" Unresolved issues become seeds planted in your heart that take root, germinate and inevitably grow into bad fruit. Fruit such as insecurity, arrogance, pride, anger, jealousy and unforgiveness. Ladies, life is too short not to maximize *every* moment. You are too precious to God not to be fulfilled, whole, satisfied and full of joy! Just like Cinderella knew in her heart there was more — so it is for you. You are not just a stepdaughter destined for leftovers! You are a joint heir with Christ *already* seated in heavenly places through Christ. Queen, take your throne.

Journey Note

178 *Today's Gem*

Rest in God and wait patiently for Him. Everything happens "on time" in God. To everything there is a season and a time for every matter or purpose under heaven according to Ecclesiastes Chapter 3. Stop working to make things happen before their time. You don't have to promote yourself, lie, cheat or manipulate to make things happen. You won't have to fight to make it happen. In God's time, it just happens if you're in place and in your season. Time is the landing place for eternal purpose. Time is the canvas upon which eternity is painted. Just know, there's a place for your portrait of purpose in the gallery of God!

Journey Note

179 Today's Gem

Are you a woman who is controlled by her emotions? I mean, you're up one minute and down the next. When you are ruled by your emotions you are more vulnerable to respond to the desires of your flesh. The Message Bible says in Galatians 5:16, "Live freely, animated, and motivated by God's Spirit. Then you won't feed the compulsions of selfishness. There is a root of sinful, self-interest in all of us that is at odds with a free spirit. These two ways oppose each other, therefore you live according to how you feel on any given day—*unless* you are a spirit-controlled Woman!

Journey Note

180 Today's Gem

The consequences of living a facade, pretending to be what you're not and perpetrating a lie or a front is that you eventually lose sight of the truth. One day you look in the mirror and realize that you don't know the person staring back at you. Be true to yourself. How? By coming to a compassionate Father and being totally transparent about your issues, your pain, your shame and your mistakes and bad choices. God has made provision for your healing and wholeness. He has made a way of restoration. In the end, if you don't take advantage of the opportunity to make it right—guess what? It's not His fault.

Journey Note

181 *Today's Gem*

Unforgiveness is like spiritual constipation. You are so backed up with bitterness, anger, resentment and hatred that it is hard to function. You continue to live a facade because you are concerned about your image and God is more concerned with your health—your spiritual health. Your appearance is together but your soul is sick. Your money is right but your mind is tormented. You have a great job but your heart is aching. Sis, God wants to cut his wound out from the root—yes, the wound that's been covered with other wounds. Why? Because it's blocking the pathway to your promise. Take a spiritual laxative today and allow God to flush out your soul. The discomfort lasts for a moment—but the freedom will be well worth the process.

Journey Note

182 Today's Gem

How do you deal with pain? God understands that pain is not pain until you feel it. God communicates His ways and His thoughts and His mysteries through your pain. Adversity perfects character. Let it hurt not so it won't destroy you later. Why? God is putting things back in order. Often, that requires that God tear down instability, inconsistency and our way of doing things. There is purpose in your pain. You can't get to a new day without first going through the midnight of an old day. The Lord loves you so much. He wants to make you mentally stable and emotionally steadfast. Before you know it, your pain will be transformed into power.

Journey Note

183 *Today's Gem*

Desire can be a dangerous thing when the object of our desire replaces God. Have you ever wanted something or someone so badly that it made you sick? Well, noted author Michelle McKinney Hammond said, "God's prevention is God's protection. God knows that the very thing you think you can't live without is the very thing that will kill you." Colossians 3:2 states, "Set your affections on things above, not on things on the earth." To set means to take and place. Take your affections and place them on things above and beyond what your flesh craves for. How? Philippians 4:8–9 says, "Finally, sisters, whatever is true, noble, right, pure, lovely, excellent or praiseworthy—think about such things. Put what you have learned from me or seen in me into practice. And the God of peace will be with you."

Journey Note

184 *Today's Gem*

You've closed your heart so that no one else can get in! But the pain from your past is also locked in! God's love wants to melt the fortress that you've built around your heart! You will love again. You will care again. You will feel again. How? Through Christ. He longs for your entire heart. What you really need and what you really want are usually so far apart. Jesus told the woman at the well in John 4:10, "If you only knew the gift God has for you and who I am, you would ask me, and I would give you living water." God wants you to put Him at the top of your list of needs and you'll need nothing else. Why? Because when Jesus becomes your everything, you will discover that He truly satisfies your every need, want and desire.

Journey Note

185 *Today's Gem*

Bitterness can make your life unbearable. It gnaws at you. Then it turns into resentment and ultimately unforgiveness. Unfortunately, unforgiveness becomes an idol that you worship because it prevents you from moving forward. Why? Because you are stuck in your place of pain. But, sis, first you must separate the offense from the offender. Then, God will work through you to release the oil of forgiveness. Ephesians 4:31–32 says, "Get rid of all bitterness, rage, anger, brawling, and slander, along with every form of malice. Be kind and compassionate to one another, forgiving each other, just as in Christ, God forgave you." Bitterness occupies space that is created for love. So release the bitterness and receive the love for your season of giving all and getting nothing is over!

Journey Note

186 *Today's Gem*

Give your disappointment to the Lord. Psalms 62:5 says, "Find rest, O my soul, in God alone; my hope comes from him." Stop putting your trust in the limited and start believing in the God that is limitless. Through Him, all things are possible. Where there is God, there is always hope. There is also always the assurance that the best is yet to come. Listen, no person on earth can produce the peace, self-worth, validation or security you seek. God is the ultimate source of all these things our hearts crave. Psalms 23:1 states, "The Lord is my shepherd, I shall not want." I shall not want for anything! So, sis, seek the Kingdom of God, seek His righteousness and then, do nothing. God will do the rest!

Journey Note

187 Today's Gem

As children and children at heart raced to the Christmas tree, God wants you to rush to the mirror. Why? You are His treasure and you are more valuable than diamonds, emeralds, silver and gold. Even with its thorns, a rose is still a beautiful flower! You are unique and necessary to complete the bouquet arrangement that God is preparing. Yes, today is a day to celebrate, and instead of focusing on what you did not receive, what you don't have, and who you have not heard from, focus on the fact that Christ wants to give you a gift—your self-worth, your self-esteem and your value as His woman!

Journey Note

188 *Today's Gem*

Love, real love, is not easy. We often confuse love for attraction or infatuation that is that warm, fuzzy, tingly sensation in response to someone or something wonderful. But real love is often an uneven exchange of appreciation, of problems, of hopes, of disappointments, which make us realize how much life is to be cherished. A woman's deepest need is to love and be loved. To not do so is to deny our very nature and suffer the pain of being untrue to our divine design. God wants us to be available to give and receive love the way He does. Even when we don't make it easy, He keeps loving us. You don't need a reason to love. Know this: give love freely and it shall be given unto you—pressed down, shaken together and running over shall it be given back to you.

Journey Note

189 Today's Gem

We as women must find our self-worth *not* in doing, but by being! Be the nurturer. Be the life-giver. Be the enhancer. Be the reflector God designed you to be. Stop looking for love in all the wrong places, with all the wrong people and using all the wrong methods. Open your heart to receive the One who has always loved you with an everlasting love, neverending love, never judging love, unconditional love. God wants to make you complete in Him. God doesn't just want your ear—He wants your whole heart. God doesn't just want to talk to you and you to Him—He wants to commune with you. You can't earn God's love! Just receive God's love! Just believe God's love! Before you know it, you'll be so full of Him, you will be overflowing!

Journey Note

190 *Today's Gem*

God intricately and delicately formed women with emotional characteristics that differ from men. A woman cannot honestly separate her emotions from her physical state. The man who touches your body, also touches your emotions. God made you that way. You cannot make love to a man and remain emotionally untouched no matter how hard you try. You cannot give your body without giving your heart. That's why God commands us in Romans 12:1 to present our bodies a living sacrifice to Him because He also wants your whole heart. You are precious to Him but He will not share you heart with others. Proverbs 4:23 says, "Watch over your heart with all diligence, for from it flows the springs of life." Let God show you what love is today!

Journey Note

191 *Today's Gem*

Every woman has needs. It doesn't matter your age, marital status, condition of your body, emotions, spirit or mind-set. It doesn't matter how long you've been a believer in the Body of Christ—if you're a woman, you have emotional, mental, physical and spiritual needs, longings and desires. Too often, we are guilty of looking to others to meet those needs—especially those close to us. Only God can meet our deepest desires, longings and cravings for acceptance, assurance, approval and affirmation. Psalms 62:1 says, "For God alone my soul waits in silence." In Christ, you have strength for all things and through Christ you can handle anything—for you are self-sufficient in Christ's sufficiency.

Journey Note

192 Today's Gem

Striving to become "every woman" is about breaking out of self-defeating cycles of repeated patterns, behaviors, choices and habits. Becoming the woman God purposed us to be requires us to stop availing ourselves to illusions—created by denial and devastation caused by other people's madness. We must begin to manage matters of the heart. This involves perceptions, expectations, misconnects, and disconnects. Proverbs 4:23 says, "Keep and guard your heart with all vigilance and above all that you guard, for out of it flows the springs of life." Hide your insecurities in the secret place of God's security—and your issues will begin to disappear.

Journey Note

193 Today's Gem

Are you insecure? Do you maneuver or manipulate relationships into what you perceive to be your favor? What has happened to you that has caused you not to trust God to be God—even in your relationships? Well, God wants us to want Him first. God wants to fill those empty places and consume us with more of Himself. It's time to move away from being all show and no substance. Time out for being all talk and no transformation through Christ. It's time to rise above our limitations and manifest Christ in the earth! It's time to move from pain to purpose. Come on, girl-friend—God has plans for you!

Journey Note

194 Today's Gem

Sometimes, life can deal us such blows that we feel we will never recover. The winds of life toss us into uncertainties and places of discomfort that cause us to feel overwhelmed. But Psalms 61:2 declares, "When my heart is overwhelmed and fainting; lead me to the rock that is higher than I." Verse 3 says, "For you have been a shelter and a refuge for me, a strong tower against the enemy. Let me find refuge and trust in the shelter of your wings." Now, sis, pause, and *calmly* think of that." Do you need help today? Let God elevate your heart from daily distractions to lasting confidence, comfort, and consistency—*in Him!*

Journey Note

Now What Do You Do?

Thank you for sharing my journey with me to this point. As I told you in my first book, *Gems for the Journey*, coming to the end of a section does not mean that your journey is over. It simply means that your journey is about to change AGAIN. Fear not, for the Lord is with you wherever you go, sis. He has tremendous plans for you. Don't be so trapped by your past or so consumed by your future that you mismanage your now. Transition is your friend. Just be aware that transition requires transformation—change. Life is about the moments you enjoy that take your breath away. You have made it this far and you can make it the rest of the way. Inhale! Exhale! Now go and be ALL that you were created to be.

Reading Group Guide

It is imperative for us to share our journeys with one another. It's time for us to bridge the gap and begin intergenerational conversations. The older women are admonished to teach the younger women. Here are some suggestions for you to begin your discussion with others:

1. Name three things you have discovered about yourself that you did not know before you embarked upon your journey to wholeness.

2. What are the top three things you need to improve as you journey to wholeness?

3. What is your ultimate dream? What steps are you taking to make that dream a reality? If you are not taking any steps, why?

4. There are some things that have hindered your progress in the past that won't touch you in the future. Affirm for the group that you now have power over it (whatever you have survived) and intend to live a victorious life. The fact that it did not kill you means you now have power over it.

5. Share some of your favorite journal entries with the group and tell why they have such impact.

Source Notes

Unless otherwise noted, all Scripture references are taken from the Holy Bible: *The Life Application Bible* Copyright 1988, 1989, 1990, 1991, 1993, by Tyndale House Publishers, Inc. Wheaton, IL 60189. All rights reserved. Used by permission.

Verses marked AMP are taken from *The Amplified Bible, Old Testament*, Copyright 1965 and 1987 by The Zondervan Corporation, and from *The Amplified New Testament*, Copyright 1954, 1958, 1987 by The Lockman Foundation. Used by permission.

To correspond with Elder Vikki Johnson or to book her for speaking engagements:
Elder Vikki Johnson Ministries
P.O. Box 152
Mt. Rainier, MD 20712
Web site: www.eldervikkijohnson.org
E-mail: elderv@eldervikkijohnson.org